Edgar Z. Friedenberg was born in New York in 1921, and was educated at Centenary College, Stanford University, and University of Chicago. He has held teaching posts at University of Chicago, Brooklyn College, University of California at Davis, and SUNY at Buffalo. Since 1970 he has been Professor of Education at Dalhousie University. He is the author of *The Vanishing Adolescent*, *Coming of Age in America*, *The Dignity of Youth and Other Atavisms*, and many articles on psychology and education. He regularly contributes to *New York Review of Books*.

Modern Masters

BECKETT	A. Alvarez
CAMUS	Conor Cruise O'Brien
CHOMSKY	John Lyons
EINSTEIN	Jeremy Bernstein
FANON	David Caute
FREUD	Richard Wollheim
GANDHI	George Woodcock
GUEVARA	Andrew Sinclair
JOYCE	John Gross
JUNG	Anthony Storr
KAFKA	Erich Heller
LAING	Edgar Z. Friedenberg
LAWRENCE	Frank Kermode
LE CORBUSIER	Stephen Gardiner
LENIN	Robert Conquest
LÉVI-STRAUSS	Edmund Leach
LUKÁCS	George Lichtheim
MAILER	Richard Poirier
MARCUSE	Alasdair MacIntyre
MCLUHAN	Jonathan Miller
ORWELL	Raymond Williams
POPPER	Bryan Magee
PROUST	Roger Shattuck
REICH	Charles Rycroft
RUSSELL	A. J. Ayer
WEBER	Donald MacRae
WITTGENSTEIN	David Pears
YEATS	Denis Donoghue

To be followed by

ARTAUD	Martin Esslin
BARTHES	Annette Lavers
DOSTOYEVSKY	Harold Rosenberg
ELIOT	Stephen Spender
EVANS-PRITCHARD	Mary Douglas
GRAMSCI	James Joll
KEYNES	Donald Moggridge
MARX	David McLellan
MERLAU-PONTY	Hubert Dreyfus
NIETZSCHE	J. P. Stern
POUND	Donald Davie
SARTRE	Arthur C. Danto
SAUSSURE	Jonathan Culler
SCHOENBERG	Charles Rosen
SHERRINGTON	Jonathan Miller

Laing

Edgar Z. Friedenberg

Fontana/Collins

First published in Fontana 1973
Second Impression April 1975
Copyright © Edgar Z. Friedenberg 1973
Printed in Great Britain by
William Collins Sons and Co Ltd, Glasgow

Contents

Acknowledgements are due to the following for permission to quote work in copyright: to Tavistock Publications for the quotations from R. D. Laing, *Sanity, Madness and the Family, The Divided Self, Knots* and *Reason and Violence*; Penguin Books for the quotations from R. D. Laing, *The Politics of Experience* and *The Bird of Paradise*; Allen & Unwin for the quotations from Jose Ortega y Gasset, *The Revolt of the Masses;* Edward Arnold for the quotation from E. M. Forster, *Two Cheers for Democracy*; Basic Books, NY, for the quotations from Rollo May, Ernest Angel and Henri F. Ellenberger, *Existence*; Faber & Faber for the quotations from T. S. Eliot, *The Cocktail Party* and *Murder in the Cathedral*; the estate of the late Flannery O'Connor and Faber & Faber for the quotations from Flannery O'Connor, 'The Misfit', *A Good Man is Hard to Find*; Macmillan & Co. Inc. for the quotation from Max Scheler, *Ressentiment*; Oxford University Press, N.Y. for the quotation from C. Wright Mills, *The Power Elite*; and Alfred A. Knopf Inc. for the quotations from Alexis de Tocqueville, *Democracy in America.*

1 The Myth of Mental Illness

'We are all murderers and prostitutes – no matter to what culture, society, class, nation one belongs, no matter how normal, moral, or mature, one takes oneself to be.' This, Ronald D. Laing observes early in his introduction to *The Politics of Experience*, published in 1967 when, presumably, he had filled both these roles to the degree appropriate to the circumstances of his life, for just forty years. Laing was born in Glasgow in 1927 and educated in the schools and University of that city, receiving his degree of doctor of medicine in 1951. 'From 1951 to 1953,' according to the information provided in the Penguin edition of his first and most conventional book *The Divided Self* (Tavistock, 1959), 'he was a psychiatrist in the British Army, and then worked at the Glasgow Royal Mental Hospital in 1955; the Department of Psychological Medicine at the University of Glasgow in 1956; and the Tavistock Clinic 1957–61. He was director of the Langham Clinic, London, 1962–65. From 1961 until 1967 he did research into families with the Tavistock Institute of Human Relations, as Fellow of the Foundations Fund for Research in Psychiatry.'

If then, by 1967, Dr Laing had come to regard himself, along with the rest of mankind, as prostitute and murderer he had surely become an exceptionally well-informed one; and one whose information included a thorough and conventional psychiatric training and sixteen years of experience as a practitioner. In the course of this time he had become, along with – though on somewhat different grounds from – Dr Thomas Szasz, one of the two leading psychiatrists to base their work on a conviction that there was, in fact, no such clinical entity as mental illness. This is a viewpoint that has since gained, and continues to gain, many adherents; though it is still relatively unpopular in the psychiatric profession.

To be told, as R. D. Laing and his co-author and fellow-psychiatrist and Glaswegian Aaron Esterson assert in the rather truculent Preface to the second edition (1970) of *Sanity, Madness and the Family* (1964) that:

> We do not accept 'schizophrenia' as being a biochemical, neurophysiological, psychological fact, and we regard it as palpable error, in the present state of the evidence, to take it to be fact. Nor do we assume its existence. Nor do we adopt it as a hypothesis. We propose no model for it. (p. 12)*

is more threatening to the practice of psychiatry than classifying psychiatrists among all the other murderers and prostitutes of the world. There really are murderers; and these might even be ranked and accorded respectful recognition according to observable variations in professional competence. The task would not be simple. Is a mother who, with no tools except wit, ingenuity, and the psychic heritage left her by her own family, drives a son or daughter to suicide to be accorded more or less distinction than a President of the United States who encompasses the violent deaths of hundreds of thousands of persons he has never ever seen? The judgment is in principle possible, however difficult it might prove in practice. But if what is called mental illness is in fact a social artifact – if, indeed, the act of

* All page references are to the editions listed in the Bibliography; Penguin editions are used whenever available.

defining a person as psychotic is nothing more than a major and often final step in a lifetime of denigration and entrapment by others who are using him for their own political purposes – then the psychiatrist who consents to the definition must be a major part of the problem, never of the solution. This does not, of course, preclude a psychiatrist like, certainly, Laing himself from being helpful to a person who has fallen or been thrust into the role of mental patient. But the psychiatrist does so precisely by rejecting that 'mental patient' label and concerning himself wholly with the person the patient has become and is becoming in his dreadful, human condition.

Laing, in the statement from which I have just quoted and elsewhere, makes it quite clear that he is not denying the possibility of mental illness or even schizophrenia. What he does deny is its relevance as a characterization of life or a therapeutic tool; while the dangers attending the abuse of the concept are manifest. The noun 'psychotic' carries the same kind of implication as the word 'felon'; persons so classified certainly come to have a great deal in common after the classification has been applied, thus setting in motion the social processes that attack and confine them. It can even be shown that felons or psychotics, as groups, possess certain features in common – like wretched families or a proneness to behave extravagantly by the standards of their society – long before they are so classified; while subsequently they display other characteristics, such as anxiety, confusion, alterations in blood chemistry associated with protracted intense emotion, to a degree that serves to distinguish them from persons not so classified. All these are common enough among people who have been driven to the threshold of the insane asylum, and are probably significantly more common than among the general population – though this is a datum with which Laing has, rather curiously, refused to concern himself.

> Our question is : are the experience and behaviour that psychiatrists take as symptoms and signs of schizophrenia more socially intelligible than has come to be supposed? That is *what* we are asking. Is this a reasonable question? ...
>
> A common reaction has been to forget *our* question, and then to accuse us of not going about answering other questions adequately. Eleven cases, it is said, all women, prove nothing. There are no controls. How do you sample your data? What objective, reliable rating scales have you employed? And so on. Such criticism would be justified if we had set out to test the hypothesis that the family is a pathogenic variable in the genesis of schizophrenia. But we did not set out to do this and we have not claimed to have done so ... Would a control group help us to answer our question? After much reflection we came to the conclusion that a control group would contribute nothing to an answer to *our* question. We have not tried to quantify our data, because we could not see how this would help us to answer our question. (*SM&F*, Preface to the Second Edition, pp. 12–13)

This passage accomplishes its purpose in making Laing's focus on schizophrenia very clear. What Laing insists on as the essence of his position is that the statements and behaviour of those deemed mentally ill are by no means irrational, but sensible when viewed from the position of the person the patient has been. What the patient does and is makes sense from his point of view; even his nonsense serves a sensible strategic purpose of counter-mystifying the parents and hospital authorities who have devoted *his* life to mystifying *him*. All human beings are sensible; if what they do and say is not intelligible, it is because the observer has failed to comprehend the existential position from which they speak and act. That position, for a helpless infant and dependent child in the hands of adults who are, in their turn, confused, anxious, and unscrupulous, may be desperate indeed, and evoke behaviour that is grotesque in its desperation. But, however grotesque it may be, it is never inappropriate nor, once the relation of the patient to other persons in his world has been understood, incomprehensible. Indeed, once the pressure on the patient is lightened, much that is grotesque simply vanishes. Much earlier, Laing observed in an opening chapter of *The Divided Self*, 'Foundations for the Understanding of Psychosis':

I must confess here to a certain personal difficulty I have in being a psychiatrist, which lies behind a great deal of this book. This is that except in the case of chronic schizophrenics I have difficulty in actually discovering the 'signs and symptoms' of psychosis in persons I am myself interviewing. I used to think that this was some deficiency on my part, that I was not clever enough to get at hallucinations and delusions and so on. If I compared my experience with psychotics with the accounts given of psychosis in the standard textbooks, I found that the authors were not giving a description of the way these people behaved with me. Maybe they were right and I was wrong. Then I thought maybe they were wrong. But this is just as untenable. The following seems to be a statement of fact:

The standard texts contain the descriptions of the behaviour of people in a behavioural field that includes the psychiatrist. The behaviour of the patient is to some extent a function of the behaviour of the psychiatrist in the same behavioural field. The standard psychiatric patient is a function of the standard psychiatrist, and of the standard mental hospital. The figured base, as it were, which underscores all Bleuler's great description of schizophrenics is his remark that when all is said and done they were stranger to him than the birds in his garden. (*DS*, pp. 27–28)

In 1956, when this statement was written,[1] Laing had not yet formulated his principled rejection of the concept of psychosis; he had merely become deeply suspicious that the condition might be largely iatro- (and socio-) genic. By 1969 he had concluded that the only essential distinction between persons deemed schizophrenic and others lay in the unconscionable demands life, through the agency of their families, had laid on them, and the devastating, though appropriate, response they had made to such demands. Granted equally destructive demands, any of us might have responded in the same way, or in ways even less adaptive.

This is true, certainly; but it leaves something important out of account. What that something is may be inferred from the peculiar tone of the 1969 statement quoted above. For life is in some degree for all of us an adversary proceeding; and in a society whose basic unit is the mono-nuclear family, parents are always in some degree adversaries to their children. And an adversary proceeding is always conducted to some degree in a double bind of the kind Laing finds characteristic of human relations in the homes of his most schizoid patients. The judge is always predisposed towards the prosecution, though perhaps not decisively so, since both are part of the establishment that maintains stability and order: both work for *Regina*, who is engaged in attacking Richard Roe. And a defendant who points this out is, unless the circumstances are truly exceptional, in contempt of court; for it is indeed unlawful to insist that the judge is, by virtue of his very position as pillar of the establishment, inherently biased. The authority of the courts depends on their putative neutrality, which may not be questioned on structural grounds; particular abuses may be cited and, if proved, require a new trial in which both prosecution and defence will behave more circumspectly. The defence is forbidden to argue, however, that the court system is inherently biased because of its own place in the political and social structure. To admit this argument is to risk invalidating the courts, thereby preventing them from discharging their fundamental function of restraining socially threatening defendants. The defendants in the celebrated 'Chicago 7' conspiracy trial and their attorneys might have spared themselves much heartache, and severe – though subsequently mitigated – sentences for contempt of court, had they understood and accepted as thoroughly applicable to proceedings in courts of law what Laing tersely states as one of the fundamental principles of life in many families, in his 1968 Massey Lectures:

Rule A: Don't. Rule A.1: Rule A does not exist. Rule A.2: Do not discuss the existence or non-existence of Rules A, A.1, or A.2.[2]

In an adversary proceeding, as in life, much of the unavoidable discomfort stems from the fact that witnesses may not choose the questions they will answer.

And the very essence of successful cross-examination is the selection of questions that destroy the witness's credibility by disrupting his view of the world, so as to make sure that the judge and jury and if possible he himself will be led to reject his view of reality, thus rendering his testimony worthless. This is much more than a matter of showing that a witness is lying. A really effective trial lawyer can often manage to leave the court with the impression that the witness is too caught up in his own limited world view, confusions, and hostilities for it to even matter whether he himself believes his own testimony.

This, precisely, is what Laing asserts that the families and psychiatrists of schizoid patients do to them, while the patients' alleged schizophrenic symptoms are evidence of their efforts to maintain their own integrity under such sustained and often brutal attack. This is almost certainly correct; but it also misses a major point. A striking feature of that 1969 Preface is the similarity of Laing and Esterson's tone to that of some of their patients as quoted in their work : the allegation that 'a common reaction has been to forget *our* question, and then to accuse us of not going about answering other questions adequately'. But this sums up almost perfectly the experience of life that Laing attributes to his trapped patients.

In fact, it sums up a large part of everybody's experience of life; psychotics, psychiatrists, candidates for public office, professors of theology, and spouses, suspected, however justly, of infidelity. But this does not mean that nothing distinguishes psychotics from other persons; on the contrary, it means that something must. Not all of us go to pieces on the witness-stands of life, even when cross-examined by Perry Mason or Harriet Peterson. Most persons who come to be adjudged psychotic were reared in homes with siblings who managed to cope, at whatever cost to themselves, with the demands made on them and retain some measure of autonomy; or, at least, avoid the catastrophic loss of autonomy involved in hospitalization. Why this should be so is not, to be sure, Laing and Esterson's question. But that is no reason why it should not be one of ours. It is an important question, and one which Laing's rejection of scientifically controlled observation makes it very difficult to answer.

Since Laing at no stage appears to have regarded his patients as especially odd, he would hardly have been expected to frame this question. But the 1959 statement does not really suggest that his patients were as much like him as Laing supposed. It certainly suggests that they found him less threatening than they did most of the people they had been obliged to defend themselves against. But he may not necessarily have understood them better; as he points out at many points in his work, persons considered schizophrenic often fear being understood much more than being misunderstood. The statement, in fact, with its tone of rather dubious modesty, strongly suggests the way liberal Southern housewives of yesteryear used to commend themselves for their excellent relations with their Negro servants.

This similarity is worth examining rather closely. Although homely, it raises certain fundamental questions about the role of communication in society that are seldom faced, and that are crucial to an understanding of psychotherapy generally and especially of Laing's position with respect to it. Social stratification in any form depends for its maintenance on the creation of certain obstacles to communication between classes. These obstacles may be institutionalized formally, as in requirements that subordinates communicate with superordinates only 'through channels'; or they may take the form of the kind of selective inattention to what the subordinate is really saying that Laing correctly perceives as characteristics of the psychiatric interview. One of the most frequently cited passages in Laing's work is the account in *The Divided Self* (pp. 29 ff.) of Kraepelin's famous, or infamous, exhibition of his presumably incomprehensible psychotic patient whose comments, Laing demonstrates, are a perfectly intelligible and, indeed, rather witty put-down of Kraepelin's pomposity and insensitive handling – the verb is literal – of his patient. Kraepelin, oblivious of the young man's attack, comments, 'Although he undoubtedly understood all the questions, *he has not given us a single piece of useful information. His talk was ... only a series of disconnected sentences having no relation whatever to the general situation.*'

Laing added the italics to the portion of this statement that he wished to stress : it is important evidence for his thesis that 'The standard psychiatric patient is a function of the standard psychiatrist and of the standard mental hospital.' His case for this proposition seems, ultimately, irrefutable; the mental patient, in the hospital as in his family, finds himself barred from communication, even though capable of it, by virtue of the low status assigned him. Laing explicitly maintains that the psychiatric interview that serves as the basis for commitment to the institution is, in Harold Garfinkel's phrase, a 'degradation ceremony', which formally initiates the person into his subhuman role as patient.[3]

But if one grants, as one clearly must, the truth of this, then Laing's relatively successful efforts to communicate across the brutally-blasted gap between the normal and the certifiably insane must be viewed in the light of this truth, too. The gap between the normal and the psychotic is not a less dangerous abyss because it is largely artificial rather than natural – any more than the gap between blacks and whites is less real and threatening because it is a social artefact. Quite the contrary. A natural barrier may be a nuisance and an obstacle that serves no man's interest; breaching it is then a technical problem only. But barriers that are established and maintained at great cost and with manifestly destructive consequences to some, if not all of the people divided by them, are not passive problems; they are highly charged parts of the social dynamism. And they are erected in such a way as to threaten most effectively the people confined on the low-status side of the barrier, who understand this very well.

Laing's humane acceptance of persons otherwise deemed psychotic must, therefore, have posed characteristic problems for them of a kind that, in a period of major status dislocations throughout society, has become familiar: the problem of how to respond to the sweet-talking liberal who sincerely wants to be on your side but who cannot really imagine the amount of misery he would have to go through if he really lived there. Retaining the support of such people requires special but time-honoured social skills: it is necessary to convey to them a sense of underlying competence and self-respect and a gratitude to them for understanding and caring about the hell you are in, and wanting to help you get out of it. But at the same time, it is absolutely imperative to remember that they don't really understand it; that their image of what it must be like is almost certainly romanticized precisely because they romanticize you. The oppressiveness and inhumanity of the staff is not the only reason why life in a prison or mental hospital is miserable; an even more important reason is that the other inmates were, in fact, a pretty weird lot when they were brought there; and mistreatment, of course, is making them worse. But this is a difficult point to raise with an ally whose support for your case is predicated on the assumption that the differences between your lot and his are minimal, and largely a reflection of your present situation.

Ultimately, as Laing came to realize during the sixties, what is required is not more humane and responsive psychiatry so much as Mad Liberation. It is certainly true, as Harry Stack Sullivan noted in the admirable and much-quoted phrase with which he ushered the psychotic into our world that 'we are all more simply human than otherwise'; and Sullivan had a strong and acknowledged influence on Laing's thought. Even so, why apologize for idiosyncrasy? What merit can there be in claiming to share a species with so sane a man as Lieutenant William Calley? Meanwhile, whatever madness may be, and however it may come to be defined, there is relatively less ambiguity about the phenomenon of social subordination.

The function of social subordination in the moulding and subsequent definition of the psychotic is crucial to any understanding of Laing's conception of mental illness. I have mentioned his use of Garfinkel's conception of the 'degradation ceremony' to characterise the psychiatric admissions interview. He makes greater and equally appropriate use of the work of Erving Goffman, who undertook a year of menial work in a St Elizabeth's mental hospital to do the field work necessary for *Asylums*[4] and came, like Laing, to see the role of mental patients as essentially defined by a process of stigmatization. Yet Laing does not really come to grips with the implications of social subordination for his work. Or, at any rate, his disdain for methodological rigour as itself a form of violation of the people whose lives he is seeking to understand keeps him from really taking account of its effects.

'Eleven cases, it is said, all women, prove nothing. There are no controls.' Thus Laing and Esterson derisively echo their critics in the passage from *Sanity, Madness and the Family* quoted earlier. But the fact that all these patients are women is an especially important datum, and possible source of bias, in a study that concludes that mental illness is generated by hostile and dishonest manipulation of individuals who cannot escape the role of victim. All these young women come from families towards the lower-middle portion of the British social-class structure. So, certainly, one could infer from the life-styles depicted, though Laing characterizes one of them, and the only one about which he troubles to vouchsafe such information, as 'a middle, middle-class family'. In any case, this is the social climate in which the aspidistra, though still perhaps the biggest in the world, has turned to plastic; of tormented and self-defeating class-pretences and lethal commitment to decent appearances. These are the kinds of homes depicted in *Billy Liar*, or the slightly less raffish plays of Harold Pinter: *The Homecoming*, if not *The Birthday Party*. The language of these families, which Laing perceives, convincingly, as the instrument by which their daughters were driven mad, sounds like Pinter dialogue, almost exactly: the double-binds, the repetitions in which the meaning has suddenly become reversed by inflection, the meaningless and threatening false jollity, the moments that verge on communication that always lapse through unenlightened self-interest, the strong scent of death throughout.

This is pathology, all right; and both Pinter and Laing – who cites Kierkegaard five times in *The Divided Self* alone – take it as evidence of the sickness unto death that afflicts the total society of which these families are but microsarcophagi. But Pinter's characters seldom get hauled away as schizophrenic – there is no place to haul them to and no member of the *dramatis personae* who could be used as a reference-standard of sanity – and that is precisely the point. Nor are his characters usually passive victims; the most obviously deranged generally throb with a baleful energy and dreadful purpose and are terrifyingly, though not constructively, effective actors in the world at large.

Some of them would, no doubt, be judged psychotic in real life – and this may, or may not, be the fate indicated for the terrified young man in *The Birthday Party* who seems otherwise an archetype of the kind of victim Laing sees. Except for sex. Yet, surely, to limit his case-material to young women is to stack the evidence a bit. For, in the kinds of homes Laing depicts, the subordination of women is – or was in 1958 – a virtually unquestioned norm. Whatever was under stress in the home would unquestionably have been dumped most heavily on the daughters, who would have been expected to take it and would have found virtually no support anywhere in the culture with which to defend what might be left of their autonomy. This is not to say, of course, that women *were* subordinated to males in all the families discussed in *Sanity, Madness and the Family*. One, indeed – the 'middle, middle-class family' whom Laing calls the Kings – is a matrilineal, matriarchal, androphagous cult that would have mortified a praying mantis. The point, rather, is that in all these families the woman's role is defined as ideally passive, subservient, inauthentic, and nasty-nice about feelings, especially erotic feelings. Mrs King and her mother are like that, too, only more so; they are domineering monsters, not powerful personages who, though evil in themselves, might still have suggested possibilities of women's liberation.

It is easy to imagine how each of the eleven young women might have been driven into the mental state in which they came or were brought to Laing's attention by the kind of life they experienced in the pathogenic homes he describes. The reader feels their lives grating away at his own sanity, and none of us can judge how we might have passed such a test. The answer to Laing and Esterson's question, then, is 'Yes, the experience and behaviour that psychiatrists take as symptoms and signs of schizophrenia are more socially intelligible than has come to be supposed.' The question, however, is a relatively uninteresting one, among the range of those that might have been raised. For example, what predisposed these persons to madness, rather than other members of their households and comparable households? This is just the sort of question that *does* require scientifically controlled study; and one whose answer would quite possibly strengthen Laing's view of schizophrenia as an ascribed stigma rather than an objectively pathological state.

His disdain for a comparison between the victims and the survivors of the psychopathogenic situations he describes seems to be due to an assumption that such comparisons could only result in meaningless psychological nit-picking that would distract attention from his insistence that what is going on is a process of aggressive social degradation rather than of psychiatric diagnosis.

Since what Laing is interested in is what those deemed schizophrenic are trying to tell us about the meaning of their lives, he dismisses at the outset those *not* so deemed. A comparative study would involve him in a frustrating search for psychological differences that he is convinced do not exist. This conviction, moreover, is not an expression of sheer dogmatic stubbornness but of insight. For Laing, convinced as he is – and with good reason – that he understands why his 'schizophrenic' patients act as they do, a controlled scientific comparison between them and those who, though often just as alienated, have escaped stigmatization would be futile. To demand this would be like insisting that medical researchers make a series of carefully controlled bacteriological comparisons between the organisms found in the saliva and bloodstream of victims of scurvy and normal individuals; for scurvy is already known to be a consequence of dietary deficiency rather than of infection.[5]

Of course, such comparisons were made in the process of finding out what scurvy was. But Laing's dismissal of controlled comparison as a technique for studying the schizophrenic process probably has done a grave disservice to his own formulation. For it is unlikely that the major factors distinguishing the two groups would be found to be psychological. They are much more likely to be social, especially if Laing is right in his basic conviction. One would expect such comparisons to reveal many more instances in which individuals with similar low status and no hiding-place, though very different personalities, had been diagnosed as schizophrenic than in which individuals with similar personality structures but very different status had been so classified. Indeed, the conception of persons having similar personalities and very different social status has no operational meaning –

since behaviour takes much of its significance from the status of the actor – unless one also assumes that similar personality may be expressed in very different behaviour, which ruins any prospect for simple diagnostic categories at the outset. Had Laing, therefore, undertaken to do what his critics suggested, he might well have obtained unassailable evidence that psychiatric diagnosis is little more than a process of social manipulation.

Laing's own position, moreover, suggests that persons who are classed as schizophrenic may indeed tend to differ systematically in one aspect of personality from those who are not so classified, though not in a manner that could, of itself, be regarded as grotesque or unresponsive to reality. On the contrary, 'schizophrenics', whatever else they may be, are people who have sought to respond to other persons' reality too much too early, and have become inextricably caught up in games other people play. In this sense, the 'schizophrenic' really is more alienated than most people; other persons' conceptions of him have become more problematic than they do for those of us who are better able either to accept or reject the efforts people inevitably make to involve us in their quests for love, conquest or status.

Laing's conception of the fundamental role of the family in generating the 'experience and behaviour' in its victims that gets them classed as mad is an aspect of precisely this sort of games theory. From the beginning of his published work in *The Divided Self*, Laing makes full and effective use of Gregory Bateson's now-classic 'double-bind' theory of the origins of schizophrenia.[6] Bateson describes schizophrenia as a state of mind having its origins in the impossible demands placed by parents on children in infancy and early years. In the severely schizogenic home, anything the child does to meet the de-

mands of one parent automatically displeases the other;
but since the struggle between the spouses, though
deadly, is also covert, the child may not even claim the
relief of admitting to himself that he knows this. He thus
becomes caught up in an impossible task – his life becomes such a task, in which there is no prospect of success, only of temporary decreases in anxiety as he learns
to behave in such a way as to challenge least the processes of mystification his elders impose on him and on
one another.

The eleven families described in *Sanity, Madness and
the Family* fit this pattern perfectly; they were selected
for that reason. In each of them the parents take the
process of human growth as itself a form of insult which
challenges their opportunity to continue making demands on their daughter that express the uneasy truce
their marriage has become. These patterns, later elaborated when the victim herself – or himself – grows up
and marries, become very complicated networks of slow
and tormented human strangulation. A variety of these,
schematized into abstract poetry, constitute one of
Laing's recent published works, *Knots*.[7] In a prefatory
note dated April 1969, Laing writes:

The patterns delineated here have not yet been classified by a Linnaeus of human bondage. They are all,
perhaps, strangely familiar. In these pages I have confined myself to laying out only some of those I actually have seen. Words that come to mind to name
them are: knots, tangles, fankles, *impasses*, disjunc-
tions, whirligogs, binds. I could have remained closer
to the 'raw' data in which these patterns appear. I
could have distilled them further towards an abstract
logico-mathematical calculus. I hope they are not so

schematized that one may not refer back to the very specific experiences from which they derive; yet that they are sufficiently independent of 'content', for one to divine the final formal elegance in these webs of *maya*.

Maya plays a rather curious role in Laing's work. The text of *Sanity, Madness and the Family* begins: 'Maya is a tall, dark attractive woman of twenty-eight.' In this context it is the name of the victim in the first family in the book, who are called the Abbots. 'When his daughter was born, Mr Abbot had been reading of an excavation of a Mayan tomb. "Just the name for my little girl," he thought.' (p. 33) This remarkable bit of auctorial hindsight into Mr Abbot's state of mind *circa* 1930 does produce the desired *frisson* at his presumed necrophilia; but it is hard to see how Laing could infer that his interest in pre-Columbian cultures of the Central-American isthmus had been quite that restricted. The name is sunny enough, and seems a felicitous choice: 'Chichen-Itza' would have seemed pretentious as the given name of a British child; while 'Uxmal' would probably have been mispronounced. 'Maya' is odd enough, considering that the preface concluded with the usual statement: 'We have taken every care to preserve the anonymity of all persons involved.' Perhaps 'Miss Abbot' is actually called Palenque.

The *maya* referred to in the quoted passage from *Knots* is not, in any case, Yucatecan; but Vedantic: 'the illusion of the reality of sensory experience and of the experienced qualities and attributes of oneself', in the words of the Random House *Dictionary of the English Language*, which seem to fit Laing's usage precisely. One such 'knot', a relatively simple one, reads:

Jack does not see something.

Jill thinks Jack does see it.

Jack thinks Jack does see it and Jill does not.

Jill does not see herself what she thinks Jack does see.

Jack tells Jill
> what Jack thinks Jill does not see.

Jill realizes
> that,
>> if Jack thinks
>>> Jill does not see that,
>>> which Jill thinks she does,
>> Jack does not see what Jill thought Jack saw.

(p. 65)

The characters in *Knots*, when not referred to simply by pronouns, are consistently called Jack and Jill, presumably in intentional reference to their clumsiness and mutually self-defeating approach to their common task in life, which are in turn both part of the expression of the bind they are caught in and part of the reason they cannot escape it. If the pail and the water, too, prove to be illusory, then, presumably Jack and Jill are what the world calls schizophrenic. Fair enough, but there are happier nursery rhymes that are just as authoritative: notably that of the old woman who lived in the shoe whom generations of children have suspected knew very well what to do but chose not to do it because she wanted all those children. At a more complex but no less mythic literary level there is Alice, awakening to face her tormentors down and shrivel them by observing that they were only a pack of cards anyway. What is the source of such strength as this?

Jack and Jill, as Laing portrays them, raise a moral question – unless one believes victims have too little free

will to provide one – as well as psychological problems:
and that is the issue of complicity. For the victims of
Laing's doubly – sometimes trebly and quadruply – bind-
ing families are, to a degree, like those of confidence men;
they could not have been trapped but for their initial
willingness to go along with the game on the confidence-
man's terms. There is not much choice about this for
persons three years old or less in the hands of all-power-
ful parental con-men. But surely it is worth asking precisely what circumstances justify perpetuating such
maya for a lifetime.

It is true that this is what we do to the extent that we
remain what psychiatry calls psychotic or even neurotic.
'There was a door, and I could not open it; I could not
touch the handle,' Edward Chamberlayne, an archetypical victim with his wife Lavinia of a Laingian entrapment, wails in T. S. Eliot's 1950 play *The Cocktail
Party*.[8] But he does, they both do, and they build a
somewhat freer and truer life together. Sir Henry Harcourt-Reilly, Eliot's sardonic and mystical psychiatrist,
who does not believe in mental illness either, helps them,
beginning by inducing them to share his perception
that:

> My patients such as you are the self deceivers
> Taking infinite pains, exhausting their energy,
> Yet never quite successful

He then brings them to see:

> ... that they are mistaken
> About the nature of their illness, and lead them to
> see
> That it's not so interesting as they had imagined.

When I get as far as that, there is something to be done.

Laing, who would hardly disagree with this position, claims Eliot as an influence on his thought in *The Divided Self*:[9] and his actual encounters with patients like the Chamberlaynes might elicit from him a similar approach. But this way of writing about them has increasingly suggested a greater degree of identification with them – so great, indeed, as to jeopardize his willingness to assess the role they might be playing in contributing to their own misery and existential plight which the world calls neurosis or psychosis.

Assessment, his position clearly implies, is not of much value to those deemed mentally ill – or, rather, it is almost certainly harmful and usually hostile as well as a part of the process that has made them what they are. What is needed instead is understanding, acceptance and, especially, *authenticity* of response from the physician who must, above all else, prove trustworthy as a person. Authenticity is a key concept in Laing's view of healing.

This is not unique to Laing; though he is certainly among the pioneers in emphasizing the indispensability of the therapist's human presence as the essential factor in whatever good he may do his client. The therapist who acts, instead, as a detached technician can only reinforce his client's problems by becoming one more in the chain of powerful individuals who have not merely pretended to take an interest in him but – what is much worse – demanded that he, too, pretend that this interest is real; while all the while they both know that the therapist's response is determined essentially by his definition of himself as a psychiatrist rather than by the feelings his patient, as a person, arouses in him. Faced with this clinical detachment, the patient can only respond, in Laing's Nietzschean phrase, to the absence of the therapist's presence or, still more destructively, to the presence of his absence. Even certain of the classical analysts who began as Freud's colleagues – Sandor Ferenczi most notably – tended to share this view. Directly contrary to this approach, the ground rules for conducting encounter-group sessions are intended to ensure that the members of the group will respond openly and in an emotionally trustworthy – however unpleasant – way to one another, thus giving each other at least the experience of having been there for them.

This must however, under some circumstances, cause not only pain – which may indeed be essential to growth – but real therapeutic difficulties. For if one assumes that what people need most is the genuine and authentic response of their fellows one must ignore the strength and prevalence of evil in the world. Laing certainly does not deny that there are evil men abroad – the experiences of his patients proves that – but like all existential therapists he does in principle deny that what is worst in men is basic or original and fully authentic. To the degree that our own growth and humaneness have not been warped or stunted, each of us will be able to and will wish to support the growth and humaneness of others. This is a very appealing doctrine; but it is not self-evident and not demonstrably true. And it seems in a way inconsistent that a man whose major point is that no human behaviour is to be dismissed as simply a symptom, but that all behaviour must be viewed as sympathetically as possible as part of a personal life-plan, should operate as if those life plans that are malign must necessarily reflect serious distortion and alienation – that is, what in another frame of reference would be called symptoms of mental illness. Is there no such thing as triumphant evil, of the kind Flannery O'Connor was writing about in *A Good Man is Hard to Find*? Was the murderous but engaging hero-villain of her story of that name, whom she ironically called merely 'The Misfit', more twisted in his destructive impulses or in his sanctimonious ones? The Misfit's response to the sudden breakthrough of the grandmother's real love and acceptance is instructive, and seems authentic enough – too authentic :

'Listen lady,' he said in a high voice, 'if I had of been there I would of known and I wouldn't be like I am now.' His voice seemed about to crack and the grandmother's head cleared for an instant. She saw the man's face twisted close to her own as if she were going to cry and she murmured, 'Why you're one of my babies. You're one of my babies. You're one of my own children!' She reached out and touched him on the shoulder. The Misfit sprang back as if a snake had bitten him and shot her three times through the chest. Then he put his gun down on the ground and took off his glasses and began to clean them.

Hiram and Bobby Lee returned from the woods and stood over the ditch, looking down at the grandmother who half sat and half lay in a puddle of blood with her legs crossed under her like a child's and her face smiling up at the cloudless sky.

Without his glasses, The Misfit's eyes were red-rimmed and pale and defenseless looking. 'Take her off and thow her where you thown the others,' he said, picking up the cat that was rubbing itself against his leg.

'She was a talker, wasn't she?' Bobby Lee said, sliding down the ditch with a yodel.

'She would of been a good woman,' The Misfit said, 'if it had been somebody there to shoot her every minute of her life.'

'Some fun!' Bobby Lee said.

'Shut up, Bobby Lee,' The Misfit said. 'It's no real pleasure in life.'[10]

Of course, as the story makes clear with great economy of means, The Misfit became what he was through the cruelty and neglect that had characterized his life. Of course he would have been different had he received, instead, affection and respect from an abundant and trustworthy source; of course, this would have been better for everybody. But that is not strictly the question raised by Laing's position. Rather, one must ask whether, at the point in The Misfit's life at which Miss O'Connor's story finds him, the murderer is not the real him – the only one there is – for he didn't, in the event, become somebody else less vicious, but himself. And doesn't the self he now is require steely rejection rather than compassion – truly require it, not merely in the interests of society but as an act of simple recognition of and respect for what he now is? He and the grandmother are genuine adversaries and in view of this fact, isn't it she rather than he who is now playing games? What is finally lacking in Laing's view of the levels of reality in human personality is, I believe, an essential respect for evil and cruelty as just as real and human as love and growth. Evil, if it be a response to earlier abuse, is not a congenital characteristic of humans; but it is natural and probably inevitable, for all of us come to depend on it to make us part of what we are.

That two of Laing's more recent statements, *The Politics of Experience* (1967), and *The Politics of the Family* (1971), should both refer to politics in their titles, and consider the political aspects of two contexts not usually seen as essentially political, is an emphatic indication of the direction his thought has been taking. His work has tended towards a major conclusion that accounts for much of its influence. It is a conclusion well suited to the spirit of our age, though perhaps equally true of all ages. It is not a conclusion about personality theory or psychodynamics of individuals, but about the ways in which individuals interact. It is therefore fundamental to an understanding of the evolution of personality within the family, and of the function of psychiatry in society.

This principle is never formally stated in Laing's work; but since he applies it repeatedly in his discussion of the situations that interest him, we may infer and state it for ourselves. It is something like this: Human personality develops in each of us as we respond to the particular power situations in which we find ourselves; our personality comes to be largely defined by our customary ways of coping with the demands that impinge on us, and with the anxiety aroused by those demands and our anticipation of possible failure or punishment. This is true in part because personality, and especially the complex, idiosyncratic pattern of defences that Harry Stack Sullivan called *the self-system* tend to be quite stable. It is true also because, as Laing has come to see it, personality so rarely gets a chance to manifest itself in situations that do not involve a power struggle. There are few of these in life, and none in relationships that have become institutionalized. Indeed, social institutions develop primarily in order to impose the constraints required by those relatively more powerful upon those relatively weaker. And there is no institution of which this is truer than the family.

Each of us joins his family as its weakest member. The neonate is powerless and must accept the family as he finds it. Of all its members, the infant is least able to formulate and impose its will on the others, though this is doubtless more nearly self-evident to babies than to their parents, who find that the infant presents new problems and awakens old conflicts that often make them feel threatened. Still, the power is actually theirs. And the most important power is the power to define reality: in Harry Stack Sullivan's term in his classic *Interpersonal Theory of Psychiatry*, to validate experience.

To Laing, as to Sullivan, the way in which experience is validated or rejected by powerful others – ordinarily parents – is the key to subsequent development of personality. How the people on whom the young child is dependent for survival respond to the way he himself responds to his experiences determines very early what he will do about what he knows, or has almost learned, to be true. But the cohesion of the family – as of the church or the nation-state – depends on a consensus as to how what is actually happening is to be interpreted. The family is held together by a set of – often contradictory – tacit agreements as to who may do what to whom and how their actions may admissibly be interpreted. *Sanity, Madness and the Family* is replete with instances in which the members of a family gang up on their hospitalized daughter, destroying the progress she may be making towards understanding and expressing her own feelings about her life. They force her back to the view of herself that threatens neither their control nor their self-esteem; the very situation that led to her hospitalization in the first place. The process is rarely if ever a matter of simple contradiction or denial of her experiences; it requires a complex network of collaborative effort that results in what Laing terms 'mystification'. But reduced to its simplest form by the vigorous canons of experimental psychology, the process described is demonstrable in the familiar experiments of Muzafer Sherif, in which naïve respondents are induced to perceive a dot on a screen that is, in fact, stationary, as moving in any direction stipulated by the experimenter and his confederates, whom the subject of the experiment has been led to believe are naïve respondents like himself.

Perhaps the most interesting of the Sherif findings is his discovery that it is far more difficult to perform this feat of mystification if two naïve respondents are included in the experiment; and quite likely to fail if there are more than two. The child who, alone among men, can both see and call out that the Emperor has no clothes is rarer than the fable would lead us to suppose. It is quite likely that those severely enough injured in the family game to be sent to a mental hospital are precisely those who were bereft to an unusual degree of support within the family – not emotional support in the sense of sympathy, but simply another member of the family with enough strength and emotional resources to serve as an honest witness that things are as they are and not as the family would have them.

In Laing's earlier case studies, one is led to infer that the hospital and its psychiatric staff are usually powerless to help much in the face of the family's investment in its romance – or Grand Guignol – and the pliability that led to the patient's hospitalization in the first place. This would certainly be Laing's view at the time he wrote *The Divided Self*. Considering that the referral process actually takes place at the instance of a threatened family or of authorities anxiously trying to maintain their authority, it is likely to be the person who clings – though much too clumsily – to his authentic if defective perception of reality who will be deemed mentally ill as a way of bringing him under social control. The individual, if such he may be called, who capitulates instead to the prevailing definitions of reality on which social cohesion depends is, by those very definitions, sane, though in order to maintain this sanity he may have abandoned, or never have developed, the capacity to take note of what his senses tell him.

Nevertheless, psychiatric intervention might still perform a therapeutic function and help free the patient to live more authentically. But in doing so it would probably set him more at odds with those who had defined him as a problem while giving him the strength to deal with them in ways less destructive to them or to himself. This is what does happen with some few of those patients who come voluntarily to a therapist and find one who feels responsible to them and to his own integrity, and who is not concerned with adjusting them to meet other people's expectations. Just this possibility must have led Laing to choose to become a psychiatrist himself. But accumulated clinical experience has led him to a position far more distrustful of official psychiatry. For psychiatry itself is a social institution. As Thomas

Szasz points out, it is a special form of education, not of medicine, being the most radical procedure available for getting patients to accept a different set of answers as right. Even more than the schools, institutionalized psychiatry, operating through social definitions of mental illness which confer the power to commit and confine the patient until he is no longer regarded as threatening, is an effective means of social control and of extirpating dissenting views of reality. One need not be a Soviet poet to learn how true this is.

Laing's movement towards perceiving psychiatric diagnosis as an essentially political act is one of the major developments of his thought. In *The Divided Self* he already demonstrates that schizophrenia serves a defensive political purpose for the patient himself; it is, in Sullivan's term, his strategy for living – though a very costly one. It prevents the patient from learning by experience and surmounting the difficulties of his infancy; his life becomes lethally static. But psychosis may, at the time, nevertheless have been the most authentic of the miserable choices open to him as a helpless member of a domineering and uncomprehending social group.

In *The Divided Self*, then, Laing perceives schizophrenia as intelligible and even as functional to the schizophrenic, but still as a distinctive clinical entity. He is already aware that only persons whose peculiar personalities threaten their families and their neighbours in certain serious ways, chiefly by undermining the repressions they depend on to keep themselves and the rest of their children in line, are likely to be classed as psychotic. But he still believed that to call these people schizophrenic conveyed some meaning about their mental state; they were people whose strategies for living did, indeed, appear bizarre until you came to understand

how their weirdness served their purposes. And chief
among those purposes for all schizophrenics was the
need to confuse their assailants by producing a counter-
mystification sufficiently obscure to throw their avid
parents and guardians off the track that led to their soul,
subtly enough to avoid being interpreted and punished as
rank insubordination.

True, psychiatry usually failed to help the schizophrenic. Many psychiatrists assumed that he was beyond
the possibility of help and beyond the range of human
communication, except when shocked into rare intervals
of lucidity by insulin or electricity. But in *The Divided
Self* Laing saw this failure as innocent, or, at worst, as the
unsought if predictable result of the way psychiatrists
defined their roles and that of the patient. Having assumed that the patient spoke nonsense they did not
listen, and thus failed to learn what they might otherwise have understood, while they likewise perpetuated
the patient's sense of isolation and helplessness at the
hands of uncomprehending forces.

For a young Scottish psychiatrist writing towards the
close of the 1950s, this is going pretty far. Still, Laing is
still on the side of his own profession: a reformer, not
an attacker. His real departure came as he grew to realize that psychiatory was not failing to be helpful but
succeeding in being unhelpful: that the profession and
its categorical imperatives about human behaviour were
explicitly, if not intentionally, a part of the patient's
problem rather than its solution. This chilling insight
froze Laing's attitude towards psychiatry not only as a
form of medical service but, somewhat less rationally,
apparently as a research tool as well. As he became
aware that psychiatry is one of the most powerful devices at the service of the forces of law and order, he

seems to have lost interest in it as an instrument for investigating human character and personality.

By this time, I suspect, it would no more occur to R. D. Laing to look to the literature of psychiatry for information about the lives of troubled people that might be used to help them, than it would to consult the files of the CIA, if he could get at them, for information useful in supporting popular revolutionary movements. And this is regrettable. In both instances, this is one place that one *should* look for pertinent information, compiled and organized at great expense of effort and money, even though it was gathered for purposes one strongly opposed. A psychiatrist who has concluded, in effect, that psychiatrists invented and maintain the category of mental illness to maximize their own status and power must grant that they are likely to have learned a great deal about the dynamisms that make what they call mental illness possible. It is too difficult and dangerous to distort the truth if one does not know quite well what it is.

But, Laing argues, it is now too late in any case for their information to be of value. Psychiatry is too thoroughly compromised by the games it has been playing with – and against – its patients. It can no longer serve to distinguish the mad from the sane, for the alienist has become a part of a pervasive alienation and even the madman seems as corrupt as the neighbours and physicians who judge him. De Sade is a failed impresario; poor old Marat a friendly neighbourhood revolutionary manqué:

> From the alienated starting point of our pseudo-sanity, everything is equivocal. Our sanity is not 'true' sanity. Their madness is not 'true' madness. The madness of our patients is an artefact of the destruction

wreaked on them by us and on them by themselves.
Let no one suppose that we meet 'true' madness any
more than that we are truly sane. The madness that
we encounter in 'patients' is a gross travesty, a mock-
ery, a grotesque caricature of what the natural healing
of the estranged integration we call sanity might be.
True sanity entails, in one way or another, the dissolution of the normal ego, that false self competently
adjusted to our alienated social reality : the emergence
of the 'inner' archetypical mediators of divine power,
and through the death a rebirth, and the eventual re-
establishment of a new kind of ego-functioning, the
ego now being the servant of the divine, no longer its
betrayer. (*PE*, pp. 118–119)

This quotation is taken from one of the later essays,
'Transcendental Experience', that make up *The Politics
of Experience* and, according to Laing's Acknowledg-
ments in that volume, 'is based on a paper delivered to
the First International Congress of Social Psychiatry,
London, 1964, entitled "Transcendental Experience in
Relation to Religion and Psychosis". Reprinted in *Psychedelic Review*, Number 6, 1965.' The man who made it
could hardly have claimed any further interest in the
conventional concerns of the psychiatric profession. But
this viewpoint imposes some rather stringent limitations
on the range and applicability of Laing's thought. Not
that it is mistaken, or even warped; the passage quoted
is convincing, if somewhat feverishly rhetorical. But it
dismisses *everybody*; and, after all, who else is there?

There is a familiar old – and by current standards,
doubtless racist – joke about an indignant Southern
farmer who, searching his chicken coop one dark and
stormy night, elicits from one of its occupants the ad-

monition, 'Boss, go away, there ain't nobody here but just us chickens!' Laing's present attitude towards schizophrenia places him rather in the position of that farmer, while the disembodied voice proceeds from a suspected schizophrenic concealed among the normal occupants of the noisome and confining coop. The difference from the joke is that Laing *believes* the voice – and, in a larger sense, it may speak the truth. Chicken coops are prisons; all their occupants are in mortal danger; and, indeed, we are all more simply chicken than otherwise. Nevertheless, a practical problem remains. Whoever it was that spoke up like that is unlikely to get along with and be tolerated by his coop-mates. He is in more immediate danger than they from the farmer as well. And he cannot be rescued by being praised for his openness and authenticity in comparison to his squawking and befeathered normal peers.

Less metaphorically, whatever degree of humanity one attributes to either mental patients or their sometimes sinister mentors and custodians, the problem of being what is called mentally ill remains an objective reality, and for most such persons an extremely disagreeable one. They are, certainly as Laing sees them, frightened and unskilled players who have lost their confidence in the confidence game that their lives have become. But if this process is part of what is meant by the politics of experience, is it not likely that a part of what they need is to become better and more effective – possibly also more ruthless – politicians? This means learning to function without losing your equanimity in situations in which real power is at stake; even learning, in the cliché phrase, to do unto others before they do unto you. Political skill would give them more room in which to manipulate, thus enabling them to defend themselves better against invasion. But the price is that they become still further enmeshed in game-playing. Personal authenticity is not a political asset; and the road to effective political participation does not lead on to Nirvana. But would not most Westerners really get more satisfaction from a series of appointments in Samsara?

This Laing would apparently deny. He notes in Chapter 3 of *The Politics of Experience* called 'The Mystification of Experience' and prepared in 1964:

> The others have become installed in our hearts, and we call them ourselves. Each person, not being himself to either himself or the other, just as the other is not himself to himself or to us, in being another for another neither recognizes himself in the other, nor the other in himself. Hence being at least a double absence, haunted by the ghost of his own murdered self, no wonder modern man is addicted to other persons, and the more addicted, the less satisfied, the more lonely. (p. 62)

While a page further on, he quotes from the *Tao Teh Ching*:

> *When the great Tao is lost, spring forth benevolence and righteousness. When wisdom and sagacity arise, there are great hypocrites. When family relations are no longer harmonious, we have filial children and devoted parents.*
>
> *When a nation is in confusion and disorder, patriots are recognized.* (p. 63)

Laing's basic principle here is clear enough; what is still at issue is the divided self. He introduces this quotation from the *Tao Teh Ching* by observing that:

Once the fissure into self and ego, inner and outer, good and bad occur, all else is an infernal dance of false dualities. It has always been recognized that if you split Being down the middle, if you insist on grabbing *this* without *that*, if you cling to the good without the bad, denying the one for the other, what happens is that the dissociated evil impulse, now evil in a double sense, returns to permeate the good and turn it into itself. (p. 63)

This is surely one of the great fundamental truths on which, since the Fall if not the Creation, man has been unable to act. Indeed, the impossibility of acting on this statement is built into the statement itself: to try to *use* it to build a better world or, indeed, for any practical purpose, would be grabbing *this* without *that*, clinging to the good without the bad. The difficulty is at least as old as the *Tao Teh Ching* itself which, being filled with wisdom and sagacity, can only have been written in a time of great hypocrites, well after the great Tao had been lost. The four paradoxes from the *Book of Tao* Laing cites, which are characteristic of most of its content, suggest even more clearly than Laing allows the difficulties of constructing a politics of experience. The basic principle underlying all these aphorisms is that conscious virtue becomes indentified as such and is deliberately put into operation only after natural wholeness has been lost. But natural wholeness knows no distinction between good and evil, since it is not self-conscious enough for that; it just is, and the path away from Being is always a downward path. Had revised editions of the *Tao Teh Ching* continued to be published, the most recent edition – in format, a *Supplement to the Whole*

Earth Catalogue – might well have included such maxims as:

> When foodstuffs are no longer wholesome and pure, science devises nutritious additives.

> When men become rootless and homeless, the Boeing 747 whisks them from place to place in luxury.

Whether the source be *Genesis*, the *Tao Teh Ching*, Norman O. Brown or R. D. Laing the lesson is the same: self-consciousness, knowledge of good-and-evil, the need to live by the sweat of one's brow, the design of technology to take the drudgery out of the work – thus also fragmenting it and reducing its meaning – these are consecutive aspects of the alienation of man from his true being. Psychiatry, too, is technology – human technology – and the worst sort of meddling of all. In principle, wilful intervention in destiny *cannot* really improve man's lot, but must create more problems or worse problems than it appears to solve. Preserving the fruit of the tree of knowledge of good and evil requires added sugar, destroys the vitamin C; the fires for the kettle pollute the air; Cain rushes home, flushed from his boyish victory, and demands Abel's share of the jam as well as his own on the slice of bread he munches as he sits down to watch the six o'clock news on TV-Eden to see if his recent triumph will be reported. It is; and in the land of Nod, too; thus establishing his image in his new home – though there, east of Eden, it's the seven o'clock news. Really, there can be no end to it except the end of the world – an end, at long last, within reach of technology.

All this may be true; indeed, it seems that it can hardly be false. But it is a truth whose implications create certain logical difficulties for its adherents. For if 'once the fissure between self and ego, inner and outer, good and bad occurs, all else is an infernal dance of false dualities', then that irrevocable and potentially fatal step has already been taken in the act of recognizing that a problem exists. This puts Laing's current position as anti-psychiatrist in a rather curious light. It does not make it logically inconsistent (unless, of course, one regards psychiatrists as a natural nuisance, like mosquitoes, which ought to be tolerated until they can be controlled by organic means like withholding fees), but it swamps it in a metaphysical issue so vast that Laing's meaning is easily lost.

The crux of Laing's opposition to psychiatric diagnosis and much psychiatric practice has been that it is repressive, coercive, political rather than psychological in that it is really a means of controlling people and putting those who make nuisances of themselves out of the way or destroying their capacity to be their own obnoxious selves. Psychiatrists use insights derived from personality theory and data about the subject's psyche in order to do a more devastating job, but they are basically unconcerned with his being and quite willing to sacrifice his selfhood for political ends. *A Clockwork Orange* – a very Laingian work – develops this theme precisely.

There is no such 'condition' as 'schizophrenia', but the label is a social fact that the social fact a *political event*. (italics Laing's) This political event, occurring in the civic order of society, imposes definitions and consequences on the labelled person. It is a social prescription that rationalizes a set of social actions whereby the labelled person is annexed by others, who are legally sanctioned, medically empowered, and morally

obliged, to become responsible for the person labelled.
The person labelled is inaugurated not only into a role,
but into a career of patient, by the concerted action of
a coalition (a 'conspiracy') of family, G.P., mental
health officer, psychiatrists, nurses, psychiatric social
workers, and often fellow patients. The 'committed'
person, labelled as patient and specifically as 'schizophrenic', is degraded from full existential and legal
status as human agent and responsible person, no
longer in possession of his own definition of himself,
unable to retain his own possessions, precluded from
the exercise of his discretion as to whom he meets,
what he does. His time is no longer his own, and the
space he occupies not of his own choosing ... More
completely, more radically than anywhere else in our
society, he is invalidated as a human being. (*PE*, pp.
100–101)

This, indeed, is a statement about politics; it describes
and assesses diagnosis and commitment as political processes, and defines the patient judged schizophrenic as a
political prisoner. It is taken from Chapter 5 of *The Politics of Experience* called 'The Schizophrenic Experience'.
In writing about 'The Schizophrenic Experience' Laing
distinguishes by implication at least between good politics and bad. Psychiatry has become vicious because it is
used by the most repressive forces in society to further
political ends. This does not make it in principle impossible to envision a society in which psychiatry might be
used to liberate, although such a psychiatry would certainly abandon the diagnostic categories and the procedures based on them that it currently uses.
Such a change would certainly be difficult to effect, if
not impossible, for perfectly concrete political reasons.

The repressive forces that now control the uses to which psychiatry is put are stronger than their opponents; they pay better, and the psychiatric profession, like teaching but on a smaller and far more luxurious scale, has largely becomes the bailiwick of upwardly mobile brain-technicians more anxious to put their skills at the service of society than of their patients. Revolution does not change this, since it usually brings to power an even less secure set of politicians committed to more extreme measures of social control. But, *in principle*, Laing's argument does not exclude the possibility of psychiatric intervention to liberate the kind of person psychiatrists now commit as schizophrenic.

But his arguments in the chapters called 'The Mystification of Experience' and 'Transcendental Experience', key sections from which I have already quoted, *do* exclude this possibility. For if the psychiatrist, as soon as he accepts the duality between self and ego, inner and outer, commits himself to a set of false dualities; if our madness and our sanity are both artefacts, equally inauthentic; if authenticity is to be the sole criterion of sanity, then there may be nothing for a psychiatrist to do that will not make matters worse. Psychiatry need not be concerned with norms; and certainly, it need not endorse as supportive of decent human life the set of norms by which it usually now operates. But it must be concerned with action; with *doing* in the world so that one can continue to *be* in the world; and to that extent psychiatry is a part – a small part – of politics.

Politics is, by definition, always concerned with action, with intervention, with the formation and execution of policy. Political action cannot even begin to be considered till after the Fall. The four aphorisms from the *Tao Teh Ching* that Laing quotes, taken consecutively, record not merely the increasing alienation but the increasing politicisation of society. For politics is concerned precisely with the implementation of power and the resolution of real conflicts of interest and thus, usually, with making the best of a bad job. Lao-tze is perfectly correct in implying that politics does not become necessary until things are already seriously disturbed. In practice, this has not proved a difficult prerequiste to meet.

Again, T. S. Eliot states the position very concisely in *The Cocktail Party*, in the consolation Reilly gives to Edward and Lavinia Chamberlayne, both rather ashamed at having chosen the path back to normality rather than that toward maximum growth and self-realization:

EDWARD: Lavinia, we must make the best of a bad job.
That is what he means.

REILLY: When you find, Mr Chamberlayne
That the best of a bad job is all any of us make of it
Except of course, the saints – such as those who go
To the sanatorium – you will forget this phase
And in forgetting it will alter the condition.

We shall examine the fate of 'the saints – such as those who go to the sanatorium' later, in considering Laing's existentialism. For the rest of us, who feel that we desperately need help in dealing with our relationship to the society and the reality of which we are a part, the issues remain, I fear, much as Freud found them to be in *Civilisation and its Discontents*. The conduct of daily life in complex organised societies depends on institutions that are sustained by myths and fuelled by the energies derived from the renunciation practised by individuals who have been led to believe in them, always at a loss to their immediate interests. What they get in return is membership, at levels providing varying degrees of satisfaction, in the social enterprise, and a variable share in what it defines as valuable. Whether their life is thereby made more worth living or less is probably impossible to answer, since only they could possibly know, and they have been driven to give the answers the society demands – not as truths but as shibboleths – and to value the rewards it offers by the very processes that Laing describes. Living, in short, turns out to be in many respects a political process, in which those who still retain some access to their feelings experience moments of self-realisation. Psychiatry can sometimes increase the depth and frequency of such moments. But the conditions under which it can do so are themselves politically influenced; and the experience is felt as something less than that of fully authentic personal transcendence. Dionysian exuberance may be increasingly tolerated in contemporary political life; but Promethean defiance still leads to serious trouble for the liver. So, at least, I should interpret the message of Herbert Marcuse.

Peter Mezan, in the *Esquire* interview cited earlier, quotes Laing as having been 'very influenced' by William James, whose *Varieties of Religious Experience is* the source of the title *The Divided Self*. But Laing's perception of what is real and fundamental in life as distinguished from what is false and trivial bears a curious resemblance, instead, to that of William's brother, Henry. The similarity is paradoxical, in view of the contrasting images and life-styles of the two men. Laing is thought of as a major exponent of openness and spontaneity in human expression; James as stylish and snobbish, elaborately reticulate in thought and writing, polished and formal – a man whom it is not only difficult but disagreeable to imagine undressed. James, the lifelong bachelor, clubman and socialite has little in common with Laing, 'A householder in Belsize Park Gardens with my wife and two children' – and five more living with his first wife in Glasgow.[2]

Nevertheless, the two share a common scorn for the external circumstances of life, regarding them as intrusions on man's subjectivity. James, as critics of his novels have frequently complained, ignores them. He deals in overscrupulous detail and ruthless honesty with his characters' feelings, perceptions, growth and decay, but taking very little interest in those aspects of their lives, especially work, by which most people feel their identity to be defined. This, as much as any attitude he ever expressed, is responsible for his reputation as a snob, since it limits his literary scope to those who are free, economically and psychologically, to govern their actions by their own motives rather than allowing themselves to be governed by external circumstances – which means, with rare exceptions, upper-status people.

Laing certainly does not ignore the effect of external circumstances and constraints on the lives of the people he treats or discusses in his work. On the contrary, their consequences are what concern him. But he writes of external reality as if it had no right to be there; the basic responsibility of the growing human being is to become himself in spite of it.

49

'Because, finally, you see, I think it's possible just to have a change of mind ... *nevertheless*. The *nevertheless* is very important. Sooner or later you have to say it – you must just get on with it, *nevertheless*. ...
What were those lines of Blake's? :

"The Angel that presided o'er my birth Said : 'Little creature, formed of Joy and mirth
Go, live without the help of anything on earth.' "

Laing smiles, picking at the carpet, and shakes his head. "I can quote that, but I would never have had the nerve to write it." [3]

In Ibsen's *Peer Gynt*, the Troll King, as I remember, stated that the maxim by which the complete Troll sought to perfect himself was, 'To thine own self, be enough'; in contrast to the human injunction 'To thine own self, be true.' It is clearly this latter injunction which lies at the heart of Laing's teaching. But in his corrosive denigration of most relationships fostered by modern society – and, especially, of those psychiatry offers its patients – he seems to accept the first as well. Neither, in any case, will serve very well as a guide to the conduct of political affairs. The recognition of the politicisation of modern life implied in the titles of Laing's works is intended, I would judge, to convey his distaste for politics; and his own political activities appear to have been minimal for a man whose writings have made him a major idol of the counter-culture during a period notable for political expression. ' "I was never *political* in an activist sense," ' Mezan quotes him as saying in the *Esquire* interview. "I suppose when people think of me as political they're thinking mainly of the Dialectics of Liberation Congress." (This was a marathon symposium, organized by Laing's colleagues, Leon Redler and Joseph Berke, which was held in London in July, 1967. Laing participated along with Marcuse, Gregory Bateson, Lucien Goldmann, Paul Goodman, John Gerassi, Allen Ginsberg, Francis Huxley, Stokely Carmichael, and others in two weeks of discussion and political analysis.) "I guess I identified myself with the Left by being there, but even at the time I made it clear that I really had no idea what could come of such an extraordinary conglomeration of people. Politically, I think I'm neutral really. I engage in no strictly *political* actions – except in the sense of following the *Tao*." '

To follow the *Tao* is to lead an essentially apolitical, rather than a politically neutral life; though this, in a society dominated by liberal interventionists intent on perfecting the world if they have to destroy it in the process, may certainly, as Laing implies, be a politically momentous stance, and perhaps the only one that makes sense. Laing is surely correct in viewing his ascribed status as a Left-activist ironically, as he is in recognizing his kinship to T. S. Eliot. The confusion – which he clearly does not share – of those who lump together as left-political quasi-revolutionary compeers persons who criticise society primarily because it alienates people from themselves and their capacities for growth, and critics who complain primarily of society's gross inequities, has caused a great deal of difficulty in the past few years. It seems to be straightening out, now, with those who are most disturbed by alienation and repression being increasingly stigmatized as reactionary by political activists and self-styled revolutionaries. The extraordinarily hostile reviews which Charles Reich's *The Greening of America* received from the American Left as well as the Right; the current split in the free-school movement exemplified by Jonathan Kozol's attack in *Free Schools* on rich liberals who set up schools in beautiful farmlands where privileged white children learn leatherwork and grooving instead of working to overthrow oppressive urban school systems; and the fairly generalised current put-down of the counter-culture as wilfully self-indulgent are all examples that suggest that the polarisation of dissent may finally be taking place on rational political grounds.

Those who try to follow the *Tao*, however, are surely more radical in their rejection of contemporary Western societies – and for reasons that would extend even to China and Japan, as highly bureaucratised, production-oriented states – than the most ardent revolutionaries bent on structural reorganisation and the seizure of power in the name of greater justice and equality of opportunity, who nevertheless leave the basic values of the society intact. The cry, 'Power to the People' exalts power as much as any statement made by those accustomed to its exercises. In this sense, Laing is anything but politically irrelevant.

For the present, at least, Laing's interests have apparently transcended both politics and psychiatry to include most of the great Eastern religions. A large section of the Mezan interview relates Laing's detailed discussion, both with Mr Mezan and with associates in an informal seminar, of several fundamental Buddhist and Hindu texts. During the time that it occurred, he was preparing for a journey to the East, since completed, in which he planned to examine some of the psychic phenomena associated with mystical states of awareness in the light of western psychological thought and practices.

'Suppose,' he muses, 'we were to hook the olfactory tracts into the visual cortex. Might we then *see* what we now smell?' He thinks it's rather strange that we are so docile about accepting our limits, like our confinement to only five senses ... 'Or suppose you could cut off all the input, all the activity, in all the sensory tracts and areas of the brain, leaving one area of cortex – say the optical cortex – open, and then re-route all the impulses from the other areas there. You could test one area of cortex at a time. I think that would be possible to do through meditation'. It is one of the ideas he's planning to test in Ceylon – one of the reasons he's going. And, I must say, I have heard in my time more extravagant claims, met less interesting ambitions.[4]

Laing's enthusiasm for psychological research in this context contrasts strikingly with his dismissal of controlled experimentation in investigating the possible sources of mental illness. This contrast is highly suggestive. The notion that the institutionalisation of the sciences as the dominant source of intellectual authority has tended to stultify Western thought about subjective areas of experience, especially mystical experience, is familiar enough, as well as surely valid. But what if the stultification has been even more pervasive. Laing's comments – and there is no reason to suppose that he is unique in this – suggest that the authority of institutionalised science may even be stultifying scientific enquiry itself; by making science impervious to some of the issues with which it ought to be concerned and with which, except for its own ideological bias, it could deal quite easily; and by alienating its more imaginative practitioners who are turned off by the uses to which science is put in society. Western thought has increasingly tended to exclude as meaningless or trivial questions that seem unamenable to empirical study; and in doing so, may actually have imposed limits on the scope of scientific investigation which its adversaries would have been powerless to enforce. It would surely be one of the crowning ironies of history if Laing, through his journey to the East, should become a science-carrier, infecting its ancient monasteries and temples with the virus of empiricism in a way no less sympathetic a visitor could have done. Somewhere, in a weathered pagoda lost to time in the highlands of central Ceylon, the monks may, even now, be installing an electron microscope, doubtless obtainable with Ford Foundation funds, and capable of minute examination of neural tissue, just in case meditation should not prove to be enough.

Laing's sojourn in the East, however, has proved to be limited, though it did include a month spent in silent fasting in the company of a holy man.[5] By the autumn of 1972 he was in America on a successful lecture tour, raising money for the Philadelphia Association which operates several small residential treatment centres in Britain for people who, in the hands of any other psychiatrist, would be patients. Two films which Laing introduced to American audiences during this visit portray the routines of life in these sanctuaries simply and movingly: *Asylums*, directed by Peter Robinson, and *Wednesday's Child*, directed by Kenneth Loach. After his respite, Laing has clearly become re-engaged in his lifework; and in an intellectual climate that is becoming more sympathetic to his position.

Laing's fundamental argument that diagnosis of schizophrenia is a political act that is hardly affected by the patient's psychic state received strong confirmation in a

widely publicised study released by D. L. Rosenhans of
Stanford University early in 1973. Rosenhans reported[6]
an experiment in which he and seven other members of
a resarch team easily got themselves diagnosed as schizophrenic and committed to twelve different mental hospitals simply by complaining that they heard voices utter-
ing single words like 'empty' or 'thud'. Though they gave
no other false information except their names, simulated
no symptoms of mental illness, gave their true, normal
case-histories – none had ever received any previous psychiatric attention – and behaved normally in hospital,
none was recognized as sane by the hospital staff. They
were confined from 7 to 52 days – the average length of
their stay was 19 days – before being released as schizophrenics whose symptoms had temporarily abated.
Whatever they did was simply interpreted by the staff –
which, in any case, avoided even eye-contact with the
'patients' as far as possible – as mad: one nurse, for
example, recorded periodically on the chart of one research worker who was keeping careful notes on his experience that he 'engages in writing behaviour'. Moreover, one hospital that had not been included in the
original study and that boasted that nothing like this
could ever happen *there* responded to Rosenhans' warn-
ing that he would send 'pseudopatients' to enter it by
judging 41 of 193 patients recently admitted to be such
'pseudopatients' – though Rosenhans, in fact, sent no
one! Meanwhile, about a third of the *bona fide* patients
in the twelve hospitals detected the imposture almost
immediately, and made comments like 'You're not
crazy! You're a journalist or a professor; you're check-
ing up on the hospital.' While this fact does, of course,
contradict Laing's position by establishing that the *bona
fide* patients did indeed differ from normal people in

ways of which they themselves, at least, were aware, thus demonstrating that they shared some clinical condition, the Rosehans experiment confirms his thesis that hospitalisation is essentially an aggressive and undiscriminating political act, whether or not it makes use of valid clinical information.

3 Laing's Relationship to Philosophy

Popular interest in the work of R. D. Laing has centred on his contributions to psychotherapy, in several roles. Besides his distinction as a practitioner and as a theoretician he has been a notably creative administrator, the founder of therapeutic communities like Kingsley Hall which from 1965 to 1970 provided a milieu in which persons who would otherwise surely have been deemed so severely psychotic as to require committal to a mental hospital could live together on a plane of substantial equality with those who cared for them, and in many cases work their way back through their early, disabling traumata to a condition that permitted them to function adequately in ordinary life. But it is clear that Laing's interests have come to transcend – or, in the language in which his philosophical writings are couched, *depass* – psychotherapy. They go far beyond those of the clinician, as in his work with the 1967 Congress on the Dialectics of Liberation; while his recent journey to the East, of course, interrupted his psychiatric practice.

Laing's gradual withdrawal beyond the role of psychotherapist began years ago. In a sense, of course, it is implicit in his early recognition that the label 'schizophrenic' is attached to persons primarily for political rather than psychodynamic reasons. In the same year, 1964, in which he developed this view in *Sanity, Madness and the Family*, he also published, in collaboration with David Cooper, another and far more obscure work which, though by implication only, attacks the roots of the psychotherapeutic process at a much more profound level.

This book, *Reason and Violence: A Decade of Sartre's Philosophy 1950–60*[1] is a work of technical philosophy: a summary condensed to one-tenth its original length of Sartre's thought as expressed in three of his works: *Saint Genet*, *Questions of Method*, and *Critique of Dialectical Reason*. Its authenticity as such is attested by a brief Foreword by Sartre in which he recognizes the book as 'A very clear, very faithful account of my thought' and refers to 'your perfect understanding of my *La Critique de la Raison Dialectique*'. Clear, it certainly is not; the book is 'so compressed as to be virtually incomprehensible to anyone seeking an introduction to Sartre's thought', Peter Sedgwick justly comments in his essay, 'R. D. Laing: Self, Symptom and Society'.[2] But Sartre must be accepted as the final judge of its validity and it certainly raises some very serious problems for anyone who might wish to continue to devote his life to – and define it by – the practice of psychotherapy.

In *Sanity, Madness and the Family*, Laing maintains convincingly that the practice of psychotherapy is frequently a political ploy; that the diagnosis and treatment of mental illness is primarily a process of social definition rather than of healing the sick. Ironically, even in the short time since the book was published, the same criticism has come increasingly to be applied to medical practice generally, thus both blurring and underscoring the distinction Laing sought to make. But this objection, whether applied to psychiatry alone or to modern medicine generally, seems more a question of values than of metaphysics. *Sanity, Madness and the Family* does not maintain that psychiatric intervention is fruitless, but that it is often undertaken in bad faith and, as such, is destructive to the patient who finds himself stretched upon an exquisitely ill-fitting framework of social demands and manipulated in order to make him fit someone else's conception of who he is and what he should be.

But the fact that psychiatry may be used for evil purposes does not preclude its use for good ones, and certainly does not suggest that psychiatry has no proper object or sphere of influence. Much of Laing's argument in *SM&F* could be used to support the position that there is indeed such a thing as mental illness, and that much of it is iatrogenic, though its primary source is in the family. Properly and effectively used, psychiatry might still heal people; though the basic values and distribution of power in the society make such use unlikely and the destructive processes which Laing condemns may remain the prevailing institutional form. By 1964, however, Laing had apparently concluded that a humane and liberating use of psychiatry was intrinsically impossible – indeed, a contradiction in terms – though this did not imply that an individual trained as a psychiatrist could not be helpful through his special perceptions and sensitivities if he thoroughly rejected the institutionalised roles and structures of his profession. *Reason and Violence* hardly mentions psychiatry or mental illness; but its fundamental argument would seem to make untenable the idea that humankind might institutionalise the means of its own liberation, whether by psychiatry, constitutional law, or eternal vigilance. It is true that Laing's paraphrase of Sartre is predicated on the assumption that life is lived under conditions of scarcity, with the implication that this may be an especially hellish aspect of capitalism; under socialism the outlook might be less pessimistic. But this does not really seem plausible as it becomes increasingly clear that technological advances in productivity and increasingly equitable distribution increase the scarcity of space, clean air and water, and privacy – none of which become noticeably more abundant under socialism. Laing himself notes: 'Scarcity must always be specified in its particular circumstances. Only careful research can determine the different contexts wherein scarcity is the condition of the possibility of history. In speaking of scarcity, some Marxists can often be quite dogmatic. Engels is often unintelligible and ambiguous. A form of scarcity they characteristically neglect, for instance, is the scarcity of time.'[3]

Reason and Violence itself, however, must be one of the most unintelligible works ever written; it can hardly be called ambiguous, which refers to a choice among several possible meanings rather than to the desperate search for even one. Yet it is essential to an understanding of the depth of Laing's commitment to existential philosophy, even if useless as a key to understanding how existentialism relates to the practice of psychotherapy and the concept of mental illness generally. Such an understanding is essential to an adequate comprehension of Laing's place in contemporary thought.

There is, however, an active and highly respected existential school of psychoanalytic thought, best represented in America by the work of Rollo May and his associates, which grew out of Jungian psychoanalytic theory and by the early 1940's had resulted in a number of explicitly existential papers on psychic functioning. In America, the influence of Harry Stack Sullivan was probably greater than Jung's; Laing, in any case, cites this earlier existential work in *The Divided Self*. He may be said, however, to have begun where existential psychiatry left off, inasmuch as his own existentialism seems to be carrying him right out of the profession. To understand how he reached his present position, it seems best to make a brief but fairly complicated excursion into comparative psychoanalytic thought.

Conventional psychiatry and classical psychoanalysis treat patients as persons who are hampered by defects in their perceptions of reality, which is conceived as external to them – as something they must be led to see more clearly and deal with more effectively. The seriousness of the patient's illness is to be judged by the depth and extent of the discrepancy between his subjective view of his life situation and the objectively correct assessment. It is not, of course, necessary to this view that objectivity be reified as the only valuable approach to knowledge, dismissing mysticism and poetic insight as neurotic epiphenomena having no pragmatic meaning. But it is necessary to maintain that the kind of detached, objective investigation of the individual's relationship to reality that classical psychoanalytic procedure requires is both feasible and desirable as the source of an intelligible and consistent account of who in the world the patient really is.

Such psychiatry thus seeks to excise from the inner life its grotesque, private, and unshareable aspects, while encouraging those that are shareable, socially serviceable, and, in every sense, agreeable. As this process leads to diminished anxiety there may even be a bonus in the subjective realm as the ego, somewhat relieved of the crushing demands of superego and id, lets a few more flowers bloom that could not have made it in the tangled forest overgrowth. Many people find it pleasanter to dwell in a park than a dark forest, even though the forest was once their own and in the park they share a condominium.

Or, perhaps, it would be more accurate to say that psychotherapy becomes recognized and established as a social institution only in those societies or sections of society in which people do prefer to live in parks, and believe that they possess the means to do so and to persuade or compel others to keep off the grass, refrain from littering and commit no nuisance. Certainly, systematic psychotherapy is a modern institution with no real pre-industrial counterparts, though literature, legend, and history all confirm that emotional conditions and behaviours now seen as pathogenic have been endemic throughout western civilization. Oedipus was, after all, the original Oedipus. But Tiresias was no Freud: he tried as hard as he could, with Sophocles' apparent approval, to forestall the development of insight in his client.

Earlier societies did, of course, classify and confine certain kinds of people as mad, most of whom would probably still be so regarded today. But mad did not mean mentally ill: people who created certain kinds of social problems were called mad, but with no implication that they should be given, or could profit from, medical treatment, except for persons of very high status like Lady Macbeth. Usually they were regarded as irredeemable rather than incurable. Occasionally, of course, the mad recovered their wits – as good a way of putting it as any other – and made their way out in the normal world, just as patients in mental hospitals sometimes do today. In the absence of a psychiatric board, it may have been easier.

The reasons for the development of the modern conception of the mad as sick people requiring the services and subject to the authority of a physician are surely complex and somewhat speculative; the most persuasive discussion of the question is Michel Foucault's *Madness and Civilization.*[4] Foucault perceives the category of mentally ill as emerging, along with that of the criminal, from a previously amorphous mass of people who, for whatever combination of personal, social, and demographic reasons, had become paupers, useless to society, without homes or valid social roles. What led the authorities to attempt to distinguish the mad and the criminal from the merely desperate, itinerant unemployed was industrialisation, which created a limited demand for the cheapest possible labour, and sought to satisfy it from among these wretched, dispossessed folk. They were not, however, all alike, any more than any other group proves to be when re-examined for reasons other than those that first led to their being grouped together. What was now needed was a device for classifying them according to their prospective employability. The merely desperately poor were immediately available; but the mad and the criminal were refractory elements, presently and often permanently unemployable, though sometimes subject to redemption and social utilisation. They required, or appeared to require, however, different regimes – or at least different rationales, since the regimes turned out to be similar enough in practice – for their rehabilitation. Criminals, by legal definition wilful miscreants, might be controlled and reconditioned by punishment; the insane, thought to be deprived of their wits and incapable of rational self-assertion, needed to be restored to rationality by means yet to be devised.

What seems incontestable is that, although people like those now called psychotic or neurotic have always been troubled and troublesome, the concept of mental illness and psychodynamic theories to account for its manifestations and suggest possible treatment for it did not develop until it became profitable to define people as objects to be used for the pursuit of extrinsic goals. There cannot, of course, ever have been a time when persons with the power to exploit others for their own purposes by force or guile did not do so. What is distinctively modern, and a prerequisite to the development of psychotherapy as a social function, is the assumption that this is what people are for: they are to be valued and to value themselves, according to their effectiveness as instruments. To the degree that one is mentally ill, one is *ineffective*, one's *functioning is impaired*, one's *perception of reality* becomes *distorted*, one's *energies are dissipated* in *inner conflict*, one's behaviour ceases to be *goal-directed*. Illness, mental or physical, makes men unfit to work, and keeps them from achieving at their highest level of productivity.

The concept of mental illness, and the function of psychotherapy, are therefore intimately involved with the conception of man as alienated, in the Marxian sense as well as the psychiatric. But they also depend on a more attractive assumption characteristic of the era of high capitalist liberalism: more attractive, at least, on the basis of liberal values, and perhaps intrinsically so. This is the premise that each human being is an individual person, with a selfhood of his very own and the capacity and responsibility to impose his will on his destiny. A man who regards himself as his own object for his own ends thereby achieves greater self-possession.

Psychotherapy as concept and process is suited to the needs of men in a shifting, open society in which the place of each is largely determined by individual adaptation and competitive achievement. Objectivity then becomes the watchword; knowing yourself becomes knowing what you are good for, knowing the difference between your feelings and reality. 'Where *id* was, there shall *ego* be' is one of Freud's more familiar statements of the function of psychoanalysis, meaning that the patient, through insight, would learn to mediate rationally between the demands arising from the depths of his being and the limits imposed on his actions and prospects by reality.

This is *not* counsel to surrender and adjust oneself so as to get along in life; and to interpret it so – though many comfortable therapists have – is to vulgarize Freud beyond redemption. It is, however, a counsel to be economical with one's psychic resources and wary about one's limitations and vulnerabilities. Psychoanalysis, Freud also observed, seeks to limit the patient's misery to that which life would in any case inflict, by improving his perception of and ability to deal with reality. To do this is not, certainly, to promise anybody a rose garden; but it does rather suggest that a serious and mature rose-fancier would surely admire the rose-fields of Bulgaria and prefer tilling them to risking scratches and snake-bites as he stumbled through uncharted thickets in search of wild ones that might be illusory.

Jung and his school, however, had never been so fully committed to objectivity. Harry Stack Sullivan, whom Laing recognizes as a major contributor to his own thought and who won Laing's respect for his uncanny ability to communicate with persons classed as schizophrenic – Freud would not accept psychotic patients – is in this respect an interesting transition figure. Sullivan was not quite an existentialist. Although he was far more broadly perceptive than the Freudian psychoanalysts in his understanding that everyone, however strange, possesses and is possessed by his peculiar strategy for living, Sullivan's conception of the function of psychotherapy was still conventional enough: to improve the

Laing

patient's ability to bring about changes in his relationship to society that would further his own ends, by freeing him from the shackles of his self-system and the difficulties he repeatedly got himself into through his efforts to reduce his anxiety by selective inattention to reality. The focus, then, is still on the external world as a refractory reality that the patient must learn to handle: its essence still seems, for Sullivan, more exigent than the patient's existence.

But Sullivan also broke with the classical technique in certain crucial ways. The most effective work could be done, he maintained, when the therapeutic hour was devoted to working through the patient's attitudes towards, perception of, and relationship to the therapist, rather than to dealing neutrally with childhood memories or even with the patient's currently crucial life relationships at home or at work. Classical psychoanalysis, of course, made a similar use of the transference relationship to illuminate the patient's character and personality; and Sullivan, like the Freudian analyst, was interested in the external check on the validity of his patient's perception of reality that this provided. If the patient believed that both his wife and his psychiatrist were trying to injure him, Sullivan had no way of being sure whether she was or not; but he did know whether *he* was.

But Sullivan valued what he called consensual validation – that is, the conviction shared by patient and analyst that their understanding of the patient's predicament was correct because it had been based on the relationship they shared and events that had taken place during the psychoanalytic sessions that both had observed and discussed – for reasons more basic to psychotherapy than the fact that it provided good objective verification of the therapist's hypotheses and guided him in conducting the analysis. Consensual validation, rather, was the essential process of therapy. Since the therapist could only be useful by participating – sharing, though not interfering – in the patient's existence, he must become a *participant observer*, not a detached observer, of the patient's being. This is quite a short step from the classic psychoanalytic position – no greater, really, than the thickness of a looking-glass. The consequences of taking it are much as Lewis Carroll and Jean Cocteau have portrayed them. It is perfectly possible to return to the side of the glass called reality, and even to continue to direct one's operations so that they will become effective there. What becomes more and more difficult is to believe that the glass divides the real from the unreal, or reflects more than it conceals.

'*Existentialism, in short, is the endeavour to understand man by cutting below the cleavage between subject and object which has bedeviled Western thought and science since shortly after the Renaissance,*' Rollo May observed in his introduction to his fundamental work on the relationship between existentialism and psychiatry.[5] Unlike Sullivan, May seems hardly to have impinged on Laing's awareness; he does include *Existence* in a list of nearly seventy References cited at the conclusion of the 1965 Penguin edition of *The Divided Self*, but does not mention it in the text. May, for his part, though wholly committed to existentialism, dismisses Sartre since, despite 'his major, penetrating, psychological analyses, it must be emphasized that he represents a nihilistic, subjectivist extreme in existentialism which invites misunderstanding'. May, a scant generation older than Laing, undoubtedly occupies the 'straight' position with respect to existential psychiatry, leaving Laing 'far out'. But their work shares not only a common philosophical basis which places it squarely at odds with the rationalism of conventional psychiatry, but common intellectual antecedents. Both men acknowledge the influence of the expected philosophical sources: Kierkegaard and Heidegger, Jaspers and Nietzsche. More immediately, Laing cites in *The Divided Self* the published psychiatric work of three of the five 'Translated Contributors' to *Existence*: 'Eugene Minkowski, Pioneer in Phenomenological Psychiatry', 'Ludwig Binswanger, Explorer in Existential Analysis', to whom the book is dedicated, and Roland Kuhn, whom the editors of *Existence* identify as 'the youngest of our contributors'. Other existential psychiatrists, like Medard Boss, are also extensively cited in both works.

Laing, then, at the time that he published his first book, still found himself in the brief but powerful tradition of existential psychiatry. Like all psychiatry this treats people as patients and distinguishes the psychotic from those of us who, for whatever reasons, have not gone, or come, so far. Existential psychiatry, moreover, would probably classify as psychotic the same people who would be so judged by classical psychiatry – but would also include others who, being still able to operate effectively in society, might have passed as normal.

For existential psychiatry speaks of mental illness in very different terms. It is not concerned with disordered perception of external reality, but with the falsification of the self. It is not concerned with diminished productivity but with loss of creativity; a creation is not a product, though once alienated from its creator it may be handled like one – this, as Nietzsche indicated in his notorious and misunderstood bulletin on the health of

God, is just what has happened to the universe. Existential psychiatry views anxiety not as a symptom but as 'an ontological characteristic of man, rooted in his very existence as such'.[6] Finding out how to help the patient to learn not to abandon himself in flight from anxiety remains the therapist's chief technical problem, as it is for classical psychiatry. But the purpose of this is not to restore him to usefulness or to calm him, but to restore the patient to himself. None of this implies that existential psychiatry encourages narcissism in the patient. On the contrary, it recognizes that he can only relate truly to other persons through his own subjectivity and his necessarily limited but vital sensitivity to theirs.

Existential psychiatry also takes a different view of neurotic guilt from that underlying Freudian psychoanalysis. In existential terms, this is real guilt, not just guilt-feelings. Conventional analysis, of course, also recognizes and deals with real guilt in patients, but this is conceived as the consequence of overt destructive acts or omissions, sharply distinguished from fantasies of guilt which connote inner conflict. The most crushing guilt recognized by existential psychiatry, however, stems from what one has failed to be, not usually, from what one has done – although, since it is by what they do that people fail to be, the distinction is not always easily made.

The most acutely unbearable inner conflict is then explainable, in terms of existential psychoanalysis, as that which occurs when an individual is torn between a severe threat to his identity, and the equally miserable, though duller, sense of guilt at his self-betrayal.

'Then what can we do when we can go neither back nor forward? Edward!
What can we do?'

So Lavinia Chamberlayne cries in anguish to her husband in her moment of truth in *The Cocktail Party*; and their therapist, Sir Henry Harcourt-Reilly, replies, 'You have answered your own question, though you do not know the meaning of what you have said.' But the answer does not lie in what she said at all; it lies in the fact that in despair she cried out to her husband, validating and affirming *his* existence as well as hers. Until then each had perceived the other as a kind of witch with the power to shrivel what was left of the other's identity, and no true strengths at all.

Therapy, whether existential or not, consists in leading the patient to accept a little more anxiety and explore the situation in which he feels it, assessing and recognizing the costs of his struggle to minimise it, with the hope of thereby widening his areas of free choice. From this point on, though they might still respond in much the same ways, classical and existential psychotherapists would discuss the process in somewhat different terms. Freud would, I judge, have felt that therapy was succeeding to the degree that it helped his patient get on with the business of living, to do what he required of himself. An existential therapist would be less likely to think in terms of success and failure. Rather he would feel the patient was getting better as he mastered his loneliness and despair, by strengthening his will to accept them, and becoming confident that they could not totally inundate him; that he himself could find the strength to make the demons let him be.

Both *insight* and *regression*, which are, of course, key concepts in psychoanalytic theory, play slightly but sometimes crucially different roles in Freudian and existential therapy. Regression in both systems means a return to earlier and more primitive ways of behaving and seeking satisfaction, under pressure of anxiety. But even though Freudian theory explicitly recognizes that regression in the service of the ego may be useful and healthy for the regressor, its function is not quite the same as in existential theory – indeed, not quite the same process is meant. As I understand it, the Freudian conception of regression has no moral dimensions: it is simply an inevitable consequence of anxiety which may be annoying in the same way that finding a bridge out and having to make a long detour is; in any case, it happens, in therapy as in life. Therapy, though, *is* life, and always does have a moral dimension; and in existential terms regression is a polarised concept, taking two contrasting forms. That which is closest to the Freudian usage is seen as vital to the therapeutic process. A major reason why Laing, despite his loathing for mental hospitals and the concept of the mental patient, still needed places like Kingsley Hall in which the people who came to him for treatment could be maintained is that he had learned that those who were most alienated needed a place in which they could, in effect, return to an infancy that, in the nature of the case, could not have been very pleasant, smearing and whining and puling at will so that the will might finally be recovered and accepted as their own.

'You might be able to find a road back
To a time when you were real – for you must have been real
At some time or other, before you ever knew me.
Perhaps only when you were a child.'

Lavinia crossly informs Edward earlier in *The Cocktail Party*. She is right, of course; this is a possibility, and the most humane one: regression in the service, not of the ego alone, but the true self.

But regression may also mean going 'back' as Lavinia used the word in the preceding quotation, when she said that she and Edward couldn't do it. They were fortunate in this. They had encountered Sir Henry at a moment of true existential crisis in their lives; and the encounter had barred their return to the mutual falseness in which they had embraced each other until then. This, too, would have been regression; it is also the source of existential guilt and despair, which deepens as one continues to let anxiety thrust the self out of its true orbit. This is not regression in the service of the ego, but of fixation, madness, and despair: the concomitants, Laing was to point out, of commonplace domestic life.

The concept of *insight* plays a somewhat more instrumental role in Freudian than in existential analysis – though the position of even the more conventional analysts today seems, in practice, to be approaching the existential. In Freudian usage, insight is both the consequence and the tool of an analysis that is progressing satisfactorily. As anxiety diminishes the patient gains more insight which slightly increases anxiety – though not to its previous level – but also adds to his security by allowing him to behave more rationally and become objectively more successful in attacking his problems. The result is a net loss in anxiety, still more insight, and so on. In existential terms the insight is almost wholly a sign that the patient is getting better – that is, more authentic – rather than a tool in making him so. As one becomes less false, there is less mystification, hence more insight – that is all, and it is enough. The problem, existentially conceived, has little or nothing to do with the fact that the patient does not understand himself correctly; it arises because the patient has developed a false self – what Sullivan called a self-system – which wards off insight by selective inattention to information that might provide it, but that would also sharply mobilise anxiety. Interpretation, which is a way of seeking to promote insight didactically, plays very little part in existential analysis. In fact, Carl Rogers – not a psychiatrist or explicitly committed to existentialism, but one of the century's most innovative psychotherapists, whose doctrines are based on a conception of the human condition hardly distinguishable from existentialism – specifically enjoins interpretation as counter-productive in the practice of his 'client-centred' psychotherapy. Perhaps revealingly, classical psychoanalysis has achieved some of its most remarkable successes with children as patients; though in child-analysis interpretation is sparingly used and insight, at least at the verbal level, not really a goal. These successes are sometimes partially explained on the basis that children are likely to be more accessible to therapy than adults because they have had less time to perfect their defences and are thus more flexible. But this seems unconvincing. Very small children can and do become as rigidly inaccessible as adults, and Freudian theory itself establishes the sources of adult neurosis in infancy – generally, the earlier it begins the worse it is. What seems more likely is that classical psychoanalysis is effective with children precisely because the analyst's conception of appropriate development in a child prevents him from laying so much rationality on him, and leaves more room for the emerging self.

Since, as I have indicated, existential psychiatry conceives of mental illness in terms of falsification of the self, where conventional psychiatry conceives of it as disordered perception of reality that elicits inappropriate responses, practitioners of the two schools may rank patients very differently as to the severity of their disturbance; while the anticipated consequences of therapy may, in certain cases, be startlingly different. To the existential psychiatrist, the most serious situation in which the patient can find himself is that where he is most completely trapped between his need to be and his desperate fear of anxiety. It is curious, as May points out,[7] that fear and anxiety should be regarded as similar feelings.

Fear is an emotion, like hope or pleasure, attached to a specific situation; it swiftly abates when the stimulus is removed, though it has its persuasive effects in prospect and retrospect. Anxiety is a gut and body feeling like pain and nausea, resulting from an insult to the psyche; it persists, though the conditions that inflicted it may have vanished. Perhaps it is possible, as Franklin Roosevelt supposed, to fear fear; but it is certainly impossible not to dread anxiety, once you have known it. Sullivan, in fact, insists that this dread is so potent that the depredations of the self-system – roughly what Freud would have called defence mechanisms – arise in response to small changes in what he calls the 'anxiety gradient' rather than to anxiety itself. This is important, because it implies that, instead of becoming able to bear increasing levels of anxiety as they grow used to it, as troops grow accustomed to fatigue, people will continue to shy away from insights and situations that make them feel sharply more anxious, even if the actual magnitude of the threat is not large; but will accept manipulation that constitutes a massive threat to their being, if it is done in such a way as to alarm them less severely than the consequences of resistance would. The political implications of this are obvious, and well known to government and law-enforcement officials; but Sullivan was concerned with the implication for therapy. What makes it most difficult is that people are, indeed, *apprehensive*; they don't just freak out under threat; they refuse to notice anything that might make them feel a little more threatened, which is much more of an obstacle. The fact that people cannot learn when they are panic-stricken is not usually very important, because during most eras there is enough time between panics to learn by experience and establish policy. But the fact that people often fail to take account of information that raises the anxiety level makes them more helpless than they need be.

How, then, does anybody ever learn anything that might enlarge his life and lead him into danger zones? There are two general factors to be considered. The primary one is, in existential terms, the self's strong, ingrained need to be. Violation of this need results in existential guilt, which hurts as much, though the pain is not as sharp, as anxiety does. It is, unfortunately, much harder to *apprehend*, especially in complex social situations. Everybody tenses-up involuntarily at the scent of a threat to the self; but the voice that warns us when we are betraying our own possibilities of being and becoming is still and small; it *will not* make itself heard over the din of cocktail parties or the murmur of committee meetings, when it is most needed. Remember, too, that, in order to be of any help, apprehension of self-betrayal must occur just when apprehension of increased anxiety is fighting against it; and anxiety, which hurts much sooner, usually prevails. No metaphor serves to bridge the gap between physical and psychic discomfort, but a partial idea may be conveyed by suggesting that accepting anxiety in order to avoid existential guilt is rather like refusing to take an analgesic when one is suffering from severe burns, simply because you have been told that the analgesic effects will wear off in three hours while the side effects of the analgesic will make you a little nauseated for the rest of your life. Three hours later, of course, the decision must be made again; and the nausea is not yet really severe – just cumulative.

The second, less general factor that makes learning and growth possible arises from the distinction between fear and anxiety. Few people will risk much increase in anxiety; but most will accept quite a lot of fear – an infinite amount, if the situation is arranged so that anxiety diminishes as fear increases.[8] Anxiety is the specific feeling that the self is threatened, that it may indeed be obliterated. There are many ways in which this can happen: through the shock resulting from abrupt drainage of self-esteem; or from so severe a violation of one's sense of the fitness of things that one can no longer find one's place and therefore cannot define one's boundaries; in the most serious instances, because the individual, from infancy, received so little response from other persons that his sense of self developed only precariously. As Bruno Bettelheim explained in *The Empty Fortress*,[9] the children most likely to be classed later as psychotic are those whose parents cared for their physical needs punctually and adequately but as a matter of utter routine, so that the infant, for example, never had any reason to feel that he was fed because his mother knew, or cared, that he was hungry. This proved far more destructive than neglect tempered by intermittent but real response, or even than cruelty, provided the cruelty was triggered by something the baby actually, and consistently, did, and was not just a random outburst directed at him as target.

People who have experienced severe and protracted anxiety since infancy may have developed no real sense of self to grow on; having anticipated possible obliteration at every moment of their lives. Even to get their anxiety down to a level that permits animal survival, they must falsify themselves and their perception of their place in the world. If the games they teach themselves work, each increase in prosperity adds to their burden of guilt. Every approach by a more fortunate, more real human being, however benign, is felt as a threat to their precarious and largely false identity. A person who lives by a cover story cannot risk being loved for himself, and certainly cannot let anybody move in with him. At its worst, such a plight may be an utter deadlock, in which every step the individual takes to assert himself bogs him down in further falsification and increases his despair – the more so if it succeeds than if it fails.

When this tragedy occurs it elicits one of the crucial differences in response between existential and classical psychotherapists. For under such circumstances the wish for death may be the only authentic wish the patient may have; and suicide the only authentic act of self-assertion open to him, since it is the only way the real self can attack the false self that has usurped all its potential. Suicide may be regarded as a highly authentic, though costly, act of self-assertion; but it cannot really be said to clarify the patient's perception of reality in such a way as to augment the chances of restoring him to full productivity. Freudian psychoanalysis must, therefore, like the everlasting it sometimes is, set its canons against self-slaughter; while existential analysis must, under such desperate circumstances, accept or at least respect the patient's decision; for the same rueful reasons that led Laing to observe, in a much lighter vein, that, 'For some individuals, masturbation may be the most honest act of their lives.'[10]

The truth of this is demonstrated by one of existential psychiatry's truly classic cases: Ludwig Binswanger's 'The Case of Ellen West'[11] which, in translation occupies 127 pages of *Existence*, and which Laing also cites briefly as presenting the archetype of despair.[12] The case is, I think, unlikely to arouse as much empathy today as Miss West's tragic suffering did at the time. The life-style of a Swiss bourgeoise whose anxieties focused on obesity now seems as remote as the difficulties of Antigone seem immediate; and Dr Binswanger's ponderous writing, which recalls the language of Sid Caesar as psychoanalyst, does not help bridge the gap. But it does suffice to convince the reader that 'it is not at all a question of single attacks of dread but of a constant dread ... the anxiety here is neither attached to a definite "traumatic" event, nor does it develop from and during such an event, for which reason psychoanalysis in this case could not illuminate anything or be therapeutically effective'.[13] And, in the light of this conclusion, the ending of the case history is strangely moving. Miss West has been discharged from the sanatorium as she has demanded. Her physicians are convinced that if released she will commit suicide, and have discussed their conclusion with her husband. But they are equally convinced that the risk must be taken, since, if she is retained, she must spend the rest of her life locked in a closed ward.

'On her trip Ellen is very courageous. The reason for taking it gives her strength. The glimpse into life which the trip gives her hurts her. Even more than in the institution she feels incapable of dealing with life.

The following days are more harrowing than all the previous weeks. She feels no release of tension; on the contrary, all her symptoms appear more strongly. The irregularity of her way of life upsets her completely; the reunion with her relatives only brings her illness more clearly into view. On the third day of being home she is as if transformed. At breakfast she eats butter and sugar, at noon she eats so much that – for the first time in thirteen years! – she is satisfied by her food and gets really full. At afternoon coffee, she eats chocolate creams and Easter eggs. She takes a walk with her husband, reads poems by Rilke, Storm, Goethe, and Tennyson, is amused by the first chapter of Mark Twain's *Christian Science*, is in a positively festive mood, and all heaviness seems to have fallen away from her. She writes letters, the last one a letter to the fellow patient here to whom she had become so attached. In the evening she takes a lethal dose of poison, and on the following morning she is dead. "She looked as she had never looked in life – calm and happy and peaceful." '[14]

'The Case of Ellen West' illustrates clearly enough the depth and commitment of existential psychiatry to the client's real sense of herself. It is better, she decided – and her physicians and husband accepted the decision – to feel your real selfhood for one, fatal day than to go on for years, in the ordinary way, trying to carry on existing as though one had not 'died' at all. Fortunately, for most of us, the choice is not that stark; but if it should be, it is better to affirm one's existence in a ceremonial libation, like Socrates, than to deny oneself. But can psychotherapy help a patient to accept, reveal, and celebrate himself? This is a fundamental question, and what it asks is quite different from what it may at first seem to involve. It is not a question about communication or the technical limits of psychotherapeutic intervention; rather, it concerns the nature of the social bond itself, and the fundamental character of social institutions.

I do not myself doubt that the question must be answered affirmatively, since I feel that I have experienced such help in full measure – moreover, in conventional Freudian analysis – and know many other people who believe that psychotherapy has been a source of increased freedom and self-realization for them, and who certainly behave as if this were true. Existentialism, of all philosophies, can hardly deny the weight or relevance of testimony because it is largely subjective. Yet there really are serious theoretical difficulties in arguing that psychotherapy can contribute effectively to the liberation and growth of the true self. It is quite possible that those of us who feel that it can have been deluded by a process which relieves us of painful constraint in some aspects of our being, but warps and stultifies our growth in areas less accessible to awareness.

The difficulties may arise at several levels. In principle, can people ever communicate their deeper and more fundamental feelings and perceptions of themselves and other aspects of reality to one another?

> They make noises, and think they are talking to each other;
> They make faces, and think they understand each other.
> And I'm sure that they don't.

So Celia Coplestone observes despairingly to Sir Henry

Harcourt-Reilly in *The Cocktail Party*, and he does not deny it. Later she comments on her relation to her former lover:

> And then I found we were only strangers
> And that there had been neither giving nor taking
> But that we had merely made use of each other
> Each for his purpose. That's horrible. Can we only love
> Something created by our own imagination?
> Are we all in fact unloving and unlovable?
> Then one *is* alone, and if one is alone
> Then lover and belovèd are equally unreal
> And the dreamer is no more real than his dreams.

This, as I understand it, is the crux of the thesis raised by Laing in *Reason and Violence*; though Laing proceeds to explain his – and Sartre's – position in economic terms. What he says is substantially similar to God's message to Adam and Eve about the economic circumstances they would find themselves in after their expulsion from the Garden of Eden. Man, forced by the conditions on which life is granted him to wrest his existence from recalcitrant nature must always reckon with the possibility that the next man – or he himself – may be one-too-many for her meagre bounty. True reciprocity, in which each accepts and contributes to the growth and the ends of the other, becomes impossible. In fact, it is therefore never even experienced as a possibility:

> Where reciprocity is modified by scarcity, the other is seen as excess, redundant, as the contra-man, the anti-man, another species. We see his actions, and these are the actions of the anti-man, our demonic double. We see that nothing, neither the great wild

81

beasts nor microbes, can be more terrible for man than an intelligent flesh-eating cruel species, who understands and thwarts human intelligence, and whose end is the destruction of man.

Abstract, pure, unmediated reciprocity is ruptured, therefore, by interiorized scarcity. Need and scarcity determine the Manicheistic basis of action and morals. Violence and counter-violence are perhaps contingencies, but they are contingent necessities, and the imperative consequence of any attempt to destroy this inhumanity is that in destroying in the adversary the inhumanity of the contra-man, I can only destroy in him the humanity of man, and realize in me his inhumanity. Whether I kill, torture, enslave or simply mystify, my aim is to destroy his freedom – it is an alien force, *de trop*. As long as scarcity remains our destiny, evil is irremediable, and this must be the basic to our ethic. The negative unity of interiorized scarcity in the dehumanization of reciprocity is re-exteriorized for us all in the unity of the world as common field of our oppositions, as the contradictory unit of multiple contradictory totalizations, and this unity we in turn reinteriorize in new negative unity. We are united by the fact of living in the whole world as defined by scarcity.' (*R&V*, pp. 114–15)

Although this sounds worse because it is so abstract, what Laing is referring to here does not seem very different from Hobbes' familiar strictures on the dismal and dangerous quality of life in a state of nature. The solution to the dread each must feel from the knowledge that he may at any moment be declared redundant by nature, red of tooth and claw or his neighbour, equally red of hand and spear, is much the same as Hobbes envisioned.

For Laing it is an unhappy solution in that it preserves life only at the expense of the self.

This solution Laing calls the *pledge* which permits previously isolated individuals to form a group with some hope that the group may endure for a time. 'The metamorphosis from series to group brings *hope* and *terror*, *freedom* and *violence* – all four are indissolubly united in all revolutionary activity.' (*R&V*, p. 133) The mere formation of the group is not enough to provide even minimal security, however, since groups fall apart once their immediate purpose has been achieved. As student-protest leaders ruefully discover and rediscover, groups are issue-oriented; effective political action requires a loyal, permanent cadre. The pledge provides this, or the promise of it; that is its function.

The pledge, however, is not a social contract, in Rousseau's sense, but the necessary passage from an immediate form of the group in danger of dissolution to another more reflective permanent form.... The pledge is not a subjective determination. *It is a real modification of the group* by my regulative action. It is my guarantee to the others that it is impossible for serial alterity to be introduced into the group through me. This guarantee cannot, however, annul the permanent possibility that I can "freely", that is, by my individual praxis, abandon my post, go over to the enemy. I have given my pledge against this exercise of my own freedom.... *I seek to convert my free being-in-the-group* into *an exigency that there is no way through or round* by the invention, as far as it is possible, of an inorganic, non-dialectical, rigid future.... The origin of the pledge is anxiety. Once the real menace from outside has passed, the danger to the permanence of the group is from dispersion and seriality. A reflexive fear arises.

'There is not enough fear to keep the group together now that the danger seems remote. The condition of the permanence of the group is thus the negation of the absence of fear. Fear must be reinvented. The fundamental reinvention, at the heart of the pledge, is the project of substituting a real fear, produced by the group itself, for the external fear that is becoming remote, and whose very remoteness is suspected as deceptive. And this fear as free product and corrective action of the group against serial dissolution is *terror* induced by the *violence* of common freedom. Terror is the reign in the group of absolute violence on its members.

'The essential basis for this transformation is the risk of death that each runs at the heart of the group as possible agent of dispersion.... This is the pledge. Its intelligibility is complete, since it is a question of free transcendence of elements already given, towards an objective already posited. My pledge offers him and them a guarantee and invited violence as his and their right to suppress me if I default.... While the circumstances are not particularly constraining, I can remain on a level where violence-terror, loyalty-treachery, are not experienced in ultimate form. But the fundamental structure of the pledged group is violence-terror, since I have freely consented to the possible liquidation of my person. My *right* over the other is my *obligation* to them, and contains in itself, implicitly, death as my possible destiny.' (*R&V*, pp. 135–37).

'But in the pledge group, there is liable to exist also a mortal concern for my co-member, my brother, he who is linked to me in an indissoluble bond, an eternity of presence without future. We have come out of the mud together, and now the brother, whose existence is not other than mine, depends on me as I depend on him. Let there be no mystification about having a "common nature". We are brothers because we are our own sons, our fraternity is our common invention. This fraternity is an ensemble of reciprocal and singular rights and obligations.... Indeed, all the internal conduct of individuals in pledged groups (fraternity and love as well as anger and lynching) draw their terrible power from terror itself. In this sense, each is the same for each in the unity of a common praxis, but, precisely because reciprocity is not integration; because the epicentres remain, albeit dissimulated, in mediated reciprocity ... the possibility of constraint or extermination is given at one and the same time in each reciprocal relation.' (*R&V*, pp. 138–39)

How much of this grimness is an expression of Laing's cast of mind rather than the logical consequence of his analysis is difficult to judge. Life really doesn't seem quite like that for most of us, though quite possibly because the bonds of brotherhood are getting weaker. What remains most serious, in its effect on the emerging freedom of the self, is the problem of false consciousness which also has its origins in the constraints of the brotherhood.

Groups possess two general and complementary means by which to guard themselves against the perceptions of reality and hence the insights that might lead to defection and ultimately dissolution: censorship and ideology. The Laing–Sartre formulation just discussed is genuinely helpful in explaining such apparent paradoxes as those that attend the extremely widespread use of classification of government documents. This is justified as necessary to conceal from real or potential enemies information that might be used to attack the nation-group; the classified material is thus placed under the protection of the pledge. But it is obvious that, in fact, much greater anxiety and hostility are aroused by the leaking of the classified material to unauthorized members of the group than to outsiders. The Pentagon Papers are the most striking example; Daniel Ellsberg and his colleagues were subjected to harassment and prosecution as betrayers of state secrets that were, in fact, known in Hanoi by the time they were compiled into the report that Ellsberg, more than a year later, revealed. The papers did not, in any case, deal with military secrets; their contents were embarrassing to the government rather than threatening to its military operations.

All citizens are assumed to be pledged at birth by the fact of their citizenship; and the fundamental purpose of the secrecy is not to protect them from their external enemies but to prevent them from learning things about their country that would weaken their identification with it and move Americans along the road to serial alterity and, possibly, Canada or Sweden. The primary function of censorship is not to keep information from outsiders, so as to forestall attacks on the group; but to keep it from group members, to forestall their possible apostasy. When censorship fails, loyal members are expected to indignantly refuse to listen to the news that has broken through. Good Russians bustle about Red Square, picking up and ostentatiously destroying unread the leaflets protesting against the invasion of Czechoslovakia that a few protesters have managed to distribute there. Good Americans as resolutely refuse to perceive Lieutenant Calley as anything worse than a mischievous, freckle-faced boy while the President makes it perfectly clear that, however those maimed and tortured bodies got there, Calley was more sinned against than sinning. Such events may even have a reinforcing effect on group loyalty; the pledge is reaffirmed in virtuous refusals to listen to the evidence against the group and by the condign punishment administered to its detractors, as in the beatings ritually inflicted on war-protesters by police, manual workers, and other patriots. Only the good Marxian – *tendence* Groucho – who stoutly insists 'I wouldn't join any club that would have me as a member', preserves his autonomy, though at a high cost in self-esteem and vulnerability, since his stubbornness costs him group protection and support.

Refusal to listen need not be a conscious act; in fact, it is usually not active at all, but passive. This is the prime social function of *false consciousness* – the social equivalent of Sullivan's *selective inattention* in the individual. Both protect the individual from feeling mounting anxiety, at the price of distorting his perception of reality and, worse, his awareness of his own real feelings. But the Laing-Sartre position correctly implies that except for threats emanating from the group itself against its potentially apostate members, false consciousness would not be necessary since deviant perceptions would occasion no anxiety in the perceiver, though they might in those he observed. If emperors could not punish their subjects for seeing them naked, there could be no fable about the Emperor's new clothes. And false consciousness, as it becomes systematised, is ideology: the system of beliefs by which members of a social group – it may, but need not, be a social class – develop a way of seeing, and interpreting what they see, congruent with what they have come to define as their interests; while denying, or providing no validation – perhaps even no language – for sensations that, if allowed to become perceptions and then ideas, would threaten those interests.

Ideology is a powerful force; more powerful, usually, than any evidence or even any experience that might oppose it. Argument does not prevail against ideology. But social cataclysm like military defeat or revolution so alter the previous group alignments that the pledges are broken, the sources of anxiety completely reorganized, and ideas and perceptions of reality previously denied to consciousness come trooping forwards, while old attitudes and beliefs drop away like rusted scrap from an electromagnet that has lost its power-supply. To the observer this looks like hypocrisy. But in fact, the group members who have abandoned and often reversed their positions are conscious of none. In a sense, indeed, there has been no hypocrisy, for their earlier position expressed their allegiance rather than their conviction; and a new allegiance brings new behaviour. Laing comments on this condition in a poetic passage :

When I obey an order, my freedom destroys itself freely and strips itself of its translucency to actualize, here, in my muscles, in my body at work, the freedom of the other. It is the freedom of the *other*, whether elsewhere, in the other, or lived here by me, that is signified by my action. It is the inflexible absence and absolute priority, everywhere, of interiorised alterity – everywhere except, of course, in this final other, who is other than all to the precise extent that he alone has the power to be himself.

Thus, the institution, as the reifying medium between men who have become passive, sets up the institution of a man as mediation between its own institutions. The sovereign is the reflexive synthesis of dead praxes.... The sovereign does not impose his power on an organised group but on an impotent series. He exploits the inertia of relations. *His power is not based on acceptance, but the acceptance of power is the interiorisation of the powerlessness to refuse it.* (*R&V*, p. 162)

It must not be forgotten that Laing is discussing here the development of a dialectic that, in the context of scarcity, he regards as inevitable. The question of individual integrity therefore does not really arise; and its potential influence is to be taken as negligible. In a sense personal integrity is not even a real possibility. Men who believe that they must act according to their conscience regardless of the interests and perceptions of the group to which they are pledged or the consequences to themselves are not freer than others. They are either marginal and in transition between groups, so that their behaviour anticipates their new pledge like the unusual sexual abstinence practised by those working class youths in the late Alfred Kinsey's old sample who had already identified with and were easing up into the middle class; or their independence is itself a class-characteristic, possibly associated with their affluence which makes them less afraid of scarcity.

Class polarisation in a society, however, may make sovereignty impossible. If the sovereign's 'power is not based on acceptance, but the acceptance of power is the interiorisation of the powerlessness to refuse it', then it is very evident that no sovereign reigns over either of the Brothers Berrigan, or their less celebrated but equally independent colleagues in the Peace Movement. No sovereign can, in this sense, reign over a society composed of different, if overlapping groups with partially or totally conflicting pledges. If the official pledge of allegiance administered in the schools is successfully challenged in the Supreme Court on the grounds that its compulsory administration is obnoxious to constitutionally guaranteed freedoms, the opponents of the pledge can hardly be said to have interiorised powerlessness to resist the state. If the President, foremost in the land, manifestly lacks 'the power to be himself', and has become notorious for his manifest selflessness, it seems evident that there is either no sovereignty in effect or that it cannot be lodged in official institutions.

'The *institution*,' Laing observes, 'is an inorganic unification of a serialised multiplicity. The *sovereign* is the dissolution, and synthetic reunification of exterior inorganic passivity in the organic unity of his regulative praxis.' (*R&V*, p. 161) Neither of these sounds as if it would be a pleasant thing to be. But both are necessary to ensure the persistence of the group through time. 'The institution, as rebirth of seriality and impotence, must consecrate power to assure its permanence by law. Its authority rests on inertia and seriality.' (*R&V*, p. 161) The reappearance of seriality, however, is precisely what happens, in Laing–Sartrean terms, when groups break up; it is just this dissolution of the group into a series of uncommitted members that the pledge is meant to avoid. What Laing seems to be arguing here is that if the group is to be effective over a longer time and a wider area than its founding members can assure through their pledge and mutual vigilance, it must find a way of establishing its coercive effect over newcomers who do not share the hope and terror of the original revolutionary experience. 'Gentlemen, we must all hang together or, assuredly, we will all hang separately,' one of the Founding Fathers is said to have remarked to his colleagues, in a cliché example of Laing–Sartrean praxis. But I, as a reluctant and poorly-pledged American, nearly two centuries later, can no longer remember which one said it, and don't care enough to look it up. Since newcomers cannot really be led to share the original experience with its intense and voluntary commitment, we cannot be so strongly bound by pledging. The security of the revolutionary group, which initially depended on the fervent will with which each of its members pledged their loyalty, now depends on the *weakening* of the recruit's sense of autonomous commitment, his sense of himself as 'just a number' in a situation which is, in fact, rather scornful of his commitment.

Any reader who has been through basic training in the American Army or Navy will know exactly what this means: by all accounts, recruits to any modern armed service, including the police, have similar experiences. The Armed Forces no longer assume that the recruit is in any sense a volunteer; his pledge may consist of no more than taking one step forward to avoid prosecution. The rituals of membership have therefore become rather pallid and desultory and are seldom seriously invoked. Not much effort is made to instill pride in the uniform as such; while any officer or noncom who attempts to invoke the unit's glorious history sounds too gung-ho. The phrase is precise, because the U.S. Marine Corps, which is the source of the 'gung-ho' concept, still prides itself atavistically on it and thinks of its members as volunteers even when they are not. The corps depends much more on physical brutality and what the Chinese Communists would call 'struggle' to approximate to the terror and violence from which loyalty was originally derived.

What *is* drilled into the Army and Navy recruit is acceptance of the idea that there is no way back to civilian life except by serving his period; that enthusiasm even in obeying orders will be regarded with mild disfavour, since he is now to understand that he has surrendered even the will to assent; that the response of the military command to his actions, whether approving or punitive, has already been programmed and will be totally impersonal. The possibility of mutiny or desertion is thus not averted by the building of *esprit de corps* based on a fervent pledge, but by deflating the will of the recruit and reinforcing his sense of his own seriality, which convinces him that he and his mates could not successfully form a rebellious group of their own – not only that they would be severely punished, but that they just couldn't get it together. This, indeed, is what institutions do.

This process, however, leaves a serious power vacuum. In the absence of a strong pledge, group cohesion depends on sanctions and rewards imposed on members whose identification with the group is weaker than that of its founders, and who by no means feel that they have freely consented to their possible liquidation. Hence the installation of the sovereign, as a source of 'synthetic reunification', dependent for his power on his subjects' 'interiorisation of the powerlessness to refuse it'. The progression, however, from a group cohesiveness derived from each member voluntarily pledging his very right to exist as a surety against this possible defection, to a group cohesiveness derived instead from the members' institutionalised sense of impotence, surely involves a very serious increase in individual alienation. By becoming a member of a group the individual cuts himself off by ideological means from authentic feelings and in-

sights that might threaten his brothers or his commitment to the group. But when the group becomes institutionalised and places itself under sovereignty, the individual member must cut himself off from his own sense
of self much more completely. He is led to abandon
much of his general sense of autonomy, to substitute a
pervasive feeling of powerlessness and apathy for the
tight but passionate circle of hope and terror. The circle
is now hollow.

This process may well account for the sense of falseness and alienation from others that seems to character-
ize membership in the official and semi-official institutions of modern life. The rebel, whatever his anxieties
and bizarre symptoms may be, seems likely to feel more
in touch with himself than the conventional citizen. And
it certainly explains why the modern nation-state, like
the professional association or the university itself
(among innumerable other possible examples) should
have become what Kurt Vonnegut Jr in *Cat's Cradle*
calls a *granfaloon* – that is, an artificial association of
people who accept a superficial common identity but in
fact have nothing in common. Contrasted to this are
the members of what Vonnegut calls a *karass*, who are
deeply involved in one another's destiny though, like
defendants in an American conspiracy trial, they may
never have met. Indeed, the knotty and obscure discussion of Sartre's *Critique de la Raison Dialectique* in
Reason and Violence turns out to have implications for
a wide variety of issues in public policy. But, what is
more to the immediate point, it does finally provide a
basis for Laing's great scepticism about the possibilities
of his own profession, and his growing rejection of it,
which is hard to refute.

For to an existential psychiatrist the purpose of therapeutic intervention is to support and re-establish a sense of self and personal authenticity. Not mastery of the objective environment; not effective functioning within social institutions; not freedom from the suffering caused by anxiety – though any or all of these may be concommitant outcomes of successful therapy – but personal awareness, depth of real feeling, and, above all, the conviction that one can use one's full powers, that one has the courage to be and use all one's essence in the praxis of being.

But psychiatry is an institution. Psychiatric staffs, like families, are groups, pledged to resist and stifle insights and tendencies towards human growth that might threaten their own power and expose them to attack from without. They are likewise members of the larger society, who acknowledge and are subject to its sovereignty and correspondingly convinced of their own internalised powerlessness to challenge its demands. Obviously, this is not equally true of all members of the profession, which has its own prophets and rebels like Laing himself. But it is true enough of the majority – and likely to be most true of those most influential – so that no one could expect psychiatry to practise what in existential terms might be called a programme of liberation unless he seriously misunderstood what an institution was. Nor could the family or the school serve the ends of existential growth, except by happy mischance, usually soon corrected by the routine vigilance of institutions. Mystification and manipulation are the *raisons d'être* of institutions; their members learn, for the sake of their membership, to mystify and manipulate themselves if there is nobody available from management to do it for them.

This is not quite so pessimistic a conclusion as it may

sound, for institutions are never as completely successful in their conquests of the human spirit as their strength, relative to this apparently frail adversary, would lead one to predict. Love, growth, inner strength, and *virtu* occur and sometimes triumph. They are anything but feeble; but they cannot be institutionalized. E. M. Forster in a radio broadcast made in England in 1939 and later published as the essay, 'What I Believe', puts the matter with utter clarity :

On they go – an invincible army, yet not a victorious one. The aristocrats, the elect, the chosen, the Best People – all the words that describe them are false, and all attempts to organize them fail. Again and again Authority, seeing their value, has tried to net them and utilize them as the Egyptian Priesthood or the Christian Church or the Chinese Civil Service or the Group Movement, or some other worthy stunt. But they slip through the net and are gone; when the door is shut, they are no longer in the room; their temple, as one of them remarked, is the Holiness of the Heart's Affection, and their kingdom, though they never possess it, is the wide-open world.

With this type of person knocking about, the constantly crossing one's path if one has eyes to see or hands to feel, the experiment of earthly life cannot be dismissed as a failure. But it may well be hailed as a tragedy, the tragedy being that no device has been found by which these private decencies can be transmitted to public affairs. As soon as people have power they go crooked and sometimes dotty as well, because the possession of power lifts them into a region in which normal honesty never pays.... The more highly public life is organized the lower does its morality sink; the nations of today behave to each other worse than they ever did in the past, they cheat, rob, bully and bluff, make war without notice, and kill as many women and children as possible; whereas primitive tribes were at all events restrained by taboos.[15]

The very idea of organizing and institutionalizing relationships between people – patients on the one hand, psychotherapists on the other – which would foster the kind of self-development that might be praised on existential grounds, appears then to be internally self-contradictory.

4 Some Implications of Laing's Philosophical Position

The three preceding chapters have been primarily exegetical. In each I have been concerned with some highly complex aspect of Laing's position. I have attempted to summarise, to analyse, to point out internal inconsistencies where they appear to exist, and to discuss some of the implications of his thought as it bears on those issues and areas of endeavour to which Laing has given most attention: psychotherapy and the nature of mental illness, the sickening effect of human institutions, notably the family and psychiatry itself; ultimately, man's experience of his own existence as a social being. Whether, and in whatever degree, these chapters have accurately dealt with Laing's views and their implications, the emphasis throughout has been on Laing's concerns, as these are reflected in his writings and occasional interviews.

But Laing's thought has important implications that far transcend his own published concerns. It would not, after all, be of very much significance if it did not. Which implications will seem most worth considering will, at this point, be determined more by one's own interests than by Laing's; nor is there any reason to assume that he himself would agree with inferences drawn from his work but applied in contexts beyond his chosen range. In this chapter, I shall discuss some of the ways in which Laing's writings, as I understand them, bear on such matters as the effect of class structure on society, citizenship and political behaviour. These are not subjects which Laing has emphasised in his writings, and I am not here attempting to paraphrase or elucidate his views on them. My intent is rather to show how his thinking might reasonably affect the reader's views, as they have affected my own.

One of Laing's most provocative ideas was outlined in the preceding chapter : scarcity lies at the root of human alienation. While Laing takes the idea from Sartre, who in turn elaborated it from Marxist sources, the kind of alienation that he emphasizes is quite different from the alienation Marx saw as a central condition of capitalism. Laing is concerned with psychological alienation, which deprives people of the capacity to accept or even become aware of their own feelings and respond to their own needs. Marx referred to the alienation of the worker from the fruits of his labour and the economic context in which he worked – his inability to control either his tools or his job, in neither of which he has any vested rights comparable to those of proprietorship. Both kinds of alienation proceed simultaneously in industrial societies and reinforce each other. Objective deprivation and economic insecurity create intense anxiety and lower self-esteem, making their victims unwilling or unable to take psychic risks, or tolerate their own or other persons' impulses towards growth, dissent or rebellion. Each individual's mounting sense of existential guilt and self-betrayal makes him increasingly hostile towards signs of growth, honest feeling, and self-realisation in others.

This viciously circular relationship between economic and psychic insecurity is a central social fact. It is the source of the psychological and political oppression that, like air and water pollution, we have come to accept as the emblem of life in our time, our grey badge of endurance. Not just of our time, either; Socrates was a victim of the resentful, cramped small-tradesman mentality that dominated Athens during the oligarchy; while Coriolanus, at least as Shakespeare pictured him, refused the act of ceremonial deference to the Tribunes of the Roman people required to qualify him as consul because he attributed to them the same 'bloody-mindedness' and desire to humiliate their superiors. That they *had* superiors, and not just superordinates in the organisation chart, and that he was one of them was not a proposition Coriolanus was inclined to question. That his superiority was truly existential is less evident to a modern reader; there were flaws in his own self-esteem that led him into treachery and destroyed him. What makes him a tragic hero rather than a grandiose failure is the fact that he did really know what quality was, and based his judgment on existential grounds. He despised the plebs because they were base, not because they were poor and low in status; they cringed and bullied, and nobility aroused their suspicions, not their admiration.

Nietzsche, one of Laing's major intellectual ancestors, developed a philosophical theory which accounts for the temperament of Socrates' tormentors and Coriolanus's indignant adversaries, as well as for the political posture of such contemporary figures as George B. Meany, or Spiro T. Agnew – examples, in abundance, may be drawn from any political party. He called the phenomenon *Ressentiment* and explained it in thoroughly existential terms.[1] A little later the Catholic philosopher, Max Scheler, elaborated the concept further, describing *Ressentiment* as 'A lasting mental attitude, caused by the systematic repression of certain emotions and affects which, as such, are normal components of human nature.... Their repression leads to the constant tendency to indulge in certain kinds of value delusions and corresponding value judgments ... emotions and affects primarily concerned are revenge, hatred, malice, envy, the impulse to detract, and spite.'[2] Sartre also makes extensive use of the idea, discussing the literally annihilating influence of 'men of resentment' in *Being and Nothingness*.[3]

Nietzsche, writing very early in the industrial era, discussed *Ressentiment* in terms of pre-industrial historical examples. But he, more than any man, has proved to be the prophetic moral philosopher of the modern era; and especially of the role of alienation and the cultural and political effect of the growth of industrial masses on the tone and quality of political life. He wrote, very clearly, about the twentieth century and can hardly be faulted for having done so during the nineteenth. *Ressentiment* is prevalent in all ages and all societies; but in modern industrial societies it becomes crucially important.

Modern industrial societies depend on megabureaucracies and micro-specialisation of function in order to co-ordinate and control their activities. The result, inevitably – almost by definition – is widespread and profound alienation in both Marxian and Laing–Sartrean terms; and with it, a profusion of severely *ressentient* individuals. Modern industrial societies, moreover, depend on demotic mechanisms for validating authority. They may not be at all democratic in the sense that power is widely shared among those affected by its use; in fact, they hardly ever are. But they do depend on counting votes at certain stipulated times in order to legitimate policy. Legitimate: reduce to law, codify, make uniform. No modern government can continue to rule indefinitely without elections.

But this requirement makes alienation heterodyne; it grows on its own feedback. The more alienated the members of any society become, the more they will be driven by *Ressentiment* to insist on their own formal sovereignty. Nobody is going to push *them* around. The little man can't do much about the crooks in office, but they had better not act as if they think they're any better than he is. Like spoiled children – which is, of course, yet another form of alienation – the more exploited, impotent, and dependent we feel, the more irritable, demanding, and occasionally viciously destructive we become. And most citizens of a modern, industrial society *are* alienated. The sovereign is, by definition, mad, and must be humoured.

Moreover, the wielders of power have a vested interest in keeping the sovereign people alienated; it exacerbates their paranoia, but it diminishes their insight and self-confidence, and hence their political effectiveness. Socialisation in a modern industrial state is in large measure systematic alienation – the systematic extinction of alternatives which a healthier human would perceive that he might have. There is no other way to get the jobs filled and keep people in them, whether the job be teaching school, bombing Indochina, or selling advertising. One of the most popular cliché-humorous desk signs bought by wistful – and *ressentient* – office workers reads: 'You don't have to be crazy to work here, but it helps.' The sign lies; you do have to be, and the man who bought it would know it if he weren't. Not mentally ill, but crazy. Socialisation into any society or group is alienating in some degree, for the Laing–Sartrean reasons discussed in *Reason and Violence*. But in a democratic political order, the alienated must be doubly mystified; a majority of the people must be induced to subscribe to and support their own reduction to seriality.

Alienation, moreover, tends to make people intrusive. Having an inadequate sense of their own selfhood, the alienated cannot be sensitive to the selfhood of others; they cannot really tell, and do not much care, where their lives leave off and those of the others with whom they are involved, but who seem no more real than themselves, begin. They have little capacity for empathy, which is one of the feelings that frighten them. And they have very little *sense of process*, in Rebecca West's phrase. They don't know what they themselves might have accomplished; they don't feel themselves to be good at anything in particular, and, in fact, do not raise the question of specific competence about themselves or those on whose skills they depend, if it can be avoided. 'The mass is all that,' Jose Ortega y Gasset observed in *The Revolt of the Masses*, 'which sets no value on itself – good or ill – based on specific grounds, but which feels itself "just like everybody", and nevertheless is not concerned about it; is, in fact, quite happy to feel as one with everybody else.... There exist, then, in society, operations, activities and functions of the most diverse order, which are of their very nature special, and which consequently cannot be carried out without special gifts. ... Previously these special activities were exercised by qualified minorities, or at least by those who claimed such qualification. The mass asserted no right to intervene in them; they realized that if they wished to intervene they would necessarily have to acquire those special qualities and cease being mere mass.... I believe that the political innovations of recent times signify nothing less than the political domination of the masses.... The mass believes that it has the right to impose and to give force of law to notions born in the café.... *The characteristic of the hour is that the commonplace mind, knowing itself to be commonplace, has the assurance to proclaim the rights of the commonplace and im-*

pose them wherever it will.'⁴

The characteristics Ortega attributes to the mass are precisely those of alienation; they are, essentially, psychological rather than social class characteristics, though people develop them, of course, in response to experiences that are strongly influenced by the socio-economic conditions they live under. Ortega himself was quite explicit about that:

> The division of society into masses and select minorities is, then, not a division into social classes, but into classes of men, and cannot coincide with the hierarchic separation of 'upper' and 'lower' classes ... strictly speaking, within both these social classes, there are to be found mass and genuine minority. As we shall see, a characteristic of our times is the predominance, even in groups traditionally selective, of the mass and the vulgar. Thus, in the intellectual life, which of its essence requires and presupposes qualification, one can note the progressive triumph of the pseudo-intellectual, unqualified, unqualifiable and by their very mental texture, disqualified. Similarly in the surviving groups of the 'nobility', male and female. On the other hand it is not rare to find today amongst working men ... nobly disciplined minds.⁵

By 'today', Ortega, of course, refers to 1930. But the idea he expresses already had a long intellectual history. C. Wright Mills, who was certainly no apologist for social elites, uses much the same distinction to help sustain a radical position in *The Power Elite*, and observes:

> By 1859 even John Stuart Mill was writing of 'the tyranny of the majority', and both Tocqueville and

Burckhardt anticipated the view popularized in the recent past by such political moralists as Ortega y Gasset. In a word, the transformation of public into mass – and all that this implies – has been at once one of the major trends of modern societies and one of the major factors in the collapse of that liberal optimism which determined so much of the mood of the nineteenth century.[6]

Recognition of the destructive effects of mass hegemony and the spread of alienation in society is not, therefore, peculiar to conservatives, though more common among them than among radicals; and certainly signifies no endorsement of current elites and their characteristics. What *are* those effects, however; what changes in the quality of life reveal mass hegemony? Primarily those that are most expressive of *Ressentiment*, of which I have chosen to discuss two that not only seem ubiquitous and especially oppressive, but also closely related to Laing's premise that scarcity engenders alienation.

The most striking of these, I believe, is the salience of envy as a large-scale political force. Envy, obviously, occurs and may be strong enough to be lethal, in every sort of society including those most remote in time and structure from our own. But in the United States, today, and in other societies like it, it has become a prime motivating force; and one whose primacy is taken for granted as a matter of ordinary political sense. The country is continually obsessed with the possibility that someone may be getting something for nothing.

As a rough check on the importance of envy as a political force in any society, consider the proportion of expenditure for amenities, social services, or welfare which is actually used for administrative safeguards against 'abuses' rather than to further the ends presumably sought. It is impossible to get an adequate welfare programme through any state legislature; cities are being driven bankrupt by the mounting costs of programmes too skimpy to alleviate misery. Yet these programmes are burdened by procedures to eliminate 'chiselling' that, it is clear in advance, will cost far more than the highest possible reasonable estimate of the total amount being 'chiselled' – and which, in any case, can only serve to make the poor more miserable by added harassment and delay. Most of the people now in prison are there for reasons connected in one way or another with their poverty – few rich, or even middle-class people, except occasional members of the Peace Movement, go to jail – and it costs upwards of ten thousand dollars per year to keep a man in prison. Yet the idea of offering those convicted, instead of incarceration, *half* that sum, or any sum at all, with which to try to pull their lives together is regarded as politically fantastic. Examples of this kind of thing could be multiplied indefinitely but are in any case familiar. What is crucial to understanding here is not the example but the ease with which we now assume that the state must, of course, behave in a suspicious and mean-spirited manner. Generosity would be politically disastrous and usually illegal in itself – misapplication of public funds.

Politicians, one assumes, must be realistic. But what policies will, in fact, be judged realistic depends on the values and customs established in the society. There is nothing inherently illogical in imagining a society that operated in the opposite way : in which tough, experienced old political touts warned romantic young candidates, 'Listen, if the whites on the west side ever found out there were black people in Chicago living in houses so run-down that their children are bitten by rats or die of lead poisoning, they'd insist that the city build housing for them in *their* neighbourhoods' or 'You're dead in this election if it gets out that you plan to vote against a $5000 a year guaranteed annual income for every head of a household – the people here won't stand for other folks having the kind of tough life some of them did.' Fiscally, there are no insuperable obstacles to either proposal. Yet both cut so hard across the grain of prevailing political values as to seem absurd.

The classic device for legitimating the unequal distribution of rewards in a democratic society is, of course, competition in which the same rules are applied to all the contestants and the status-system of the society is protected by the nature of the rules rather than by their inequitable application. The people in the society thus learn to divide themselves into winners and losers, and to blame themselves for being among the losers – winning isn't the most important thing, it's the only thing, as the great football coach said, though legends differ as to which one. The impartiality of the judges therefore becomes enormously important and the object of malevolent scrutiny; helping a friend becomes cheating and compassion becomes favouritism. Some important consequences of this device, by which envy is harnessed, amplified, and diverted to the ends of social control, were explicitly stated by Tocqueville in a passage from *Democracy in America* that presages the rise of the state school system – though Tocqueville did not intend it as a discussion of education :

As the candidates appear to be nearly alike, and as it is difficult to make a selection without infringing the principle of equality, which is the supreme law of democratic societies, the first idea which suggests itself is to make them all advance at the same rate and submit to the same trials. Thus, in proportion as men become more alike and the principle of equality is more peaceably and deeply infused into the institutions and manners of country, the rules for advancement become more inflexible, advancement itself slower, and the difficulty of arriving quickly at a certain height far greater. From hatred of privilege and from the embarassment of choosing, all men are at last forced, whatever may be their standard, to pass the same ordeal; all are indiscriminately subjected to a multitude of petty preliminary exercises, in which their youth is wasted and their imagination quenched, so that they despair of ever fully attaining what is held out to them; and when at length they are in a condition to perform any extraordinary acts, the taste for such things has forsaken them.[7]

Thus envy, perhaps the most divisive of emotions, becomes institutionalised in the egalitarian, industrial society as a major social force; defined, according to the value-system of that society, as constructive in its effects, though never praised in its own name. Envy even becomes the source of social cohesion : various forms of antagonistic co-operation evolve among competitors alert to protect their future interest despite their mutual antagonism; weaker competitors abandon their hostility to gang up on and eliminate a stronger. This is, *a fortiori*, the Laing–Sartrean group in formation; and the more effective the process of induction into the group, the more complete the synthetic reunification of seriality and impotence. At its most striking, the effect is to produce what Thorstein Veblen called 'trained incapacity'. The

athlete who learns cheerfully to subordinate the unique
and superior skills that make him a star to the necessities
of being a good – and non-threatening – team player is a
relatively benign example. The hospital nurse who learns
to allow a patient to die without even recalling that she
herself knows the procedure that would save his life,
though no physician can be reached in time to prescribe
it, a less benign one. Envy, as a social force, in the pre-
industrial Arab world – and for that matter, to a lesser
degree, even in early nineteenth-century Charleston – led
to a characteristic form of urban dwelling for the
affluent: a house in a large and beautiful garden, totally
concealed behind a blank wall that gave no hint of the
luxury within to arouse the passions of those excluded
from it. In Pacific Palisades or Lake Forest, the luxury is
so visible as to be self-deprecating, attesting that the
owner is a good old boy who lets it all hang out. The
blankness and banality have been internalised; there is
no longer anyone to be envied in residence.

The second salient and pervasive effect of *Ressentiment*
that reveals mass hegemony is a major change in the
prevalence – and in the very nature – of surveillance
and censorship. These, of course, occur under all forms
of tyranny; not just 'the tyranny of the majority'. But in
the old-fashioned authoritarian governments of a repressive monarchy or church, censorship and surveillance,
however heavy, were concerned directly with preventing challenges to the governing authority and very little
else. When the government perceives itself as threatened by revolutionary movements it will defend its pre-
rogatives by violence as great as that of any modern
state, limited only by available technology; and it will
suppress revolutionary ideas as firmly. But it is unlikely

to extend its repression into matters remotely related to statecraft: personal taste, sexual morality, or, apart from the treatment of overtly political topics, the arts.

An authoritarian government which is not democratic in form is under less necessity to use power obliquely; playing from a strong suit well-established as trump it has little need to finesse. But a state like a modern industrial state that depends for its successful operation on the alienation of the citizenry and for its legitimation and power on their consent, must proceed more obliquely. It cannot permit its citizens, and especially its youth, contact with experiences – either directly or mediated through the arts – that diminish their alienation, put them in touch with their real feelings and perceptions of reality, and free them from the shackles of bad faith and existential guilt at their complicity in their own alienation. Censorship and surveillance must be directed at the elimination of such experiences as well as – and usually more vigilantly than – politically inflammatory materials.

Liberal enthusiasts for successful revolutionary regimes are therefore recurrently – one would think, by now, predictably – embarrassed by the often grossly repressive puritanism of the regimes they have supported. Leaving aside the notorious and traditional hostility of the Soviet Union and its associates to subjectivity and ambiguity in any form of artistic expression – as towards psychoanalysis itself, though for reasons just the contrary of those that have led to Laing's disenchantment with it – the more recent and presumably more volatile and less old-fashioned revolutionary movements have behaved similarly virtually from the outset. The Cuban government continues to persecute homosexuals. Ontario school teachers, the local press reports, delightedly in-form the group of pupils they are about to escort on a tour of China that they will have to get their hair cut and dress modestly, since Chairman Mao has declared long hair and miniskirts to be decadent. On the smallest possible scale, tragicomically, Eldridge Cleaver executes a 'revolutionary bust' on his erstwhile friends, Timothy and Rosemary Leary, for their expressive tolerance towards psychedelic drugs, in emulation and propitiation of his Algerian hosts.

Several factors are at work here. What is paramount is the need of the new revolutionary state, short of capital itself and at odds with those who possess it, to exact from its citizens continued sacrifices that are not in their immediate interests, though they are necessary to the development of the state. The citizen must therefore be led to act as though these deprivations were in his interest – a fact he cannot personally experience, but must accept as a consequence of his pledge to the group. A democratic state, however, exacts not merely obedience and sacrifice as membership dues under the pledge; it demands enthusiasm and ratification as well. It must, at least at irregular intervals, proffer a ballot; it must also prevent that ballot from being used to actually reject the programmes or personnel that have become sovereign. There are many devices that convert the election into a ceremonial by which the voter celebrates his citizenship instead of attempting to influence the course of government. Voting is trumpeted as a patriotic act; and it is an assertion of one's membership in the group and of one's complicity in its programmes. This aspect may account for the peculiar institutional flavour of the polling place which, even in a 'silk-stocking' precinct, invariably shares the public squalor that John Kenneth Galbraith acutely ascribed to places and means of conducting public business in America. A polling place is, *par excellence*, a place where there is nothing to lead anybody to think he is any better than anybody else; it is usually in a church basement or school auditorium; if on private premises, it is set up in the garage. The clerks, characteristically, look and act like schoolteachers; they are pompously solemn as they scrutinize the registration lists under the suspicious eyes of the poll-watchers. It is difficult for a voter to enter the booth itself and swing the huge, clanking handle that sets the machine and draws the heavy curtain that conceals the upper part of the body *only*, without feeling that he is suspected of being about to commit an indecent act; though, even if the curtain were longer, hardly anyone could masturbate successfully in a polling-place. The *ambience* is *Ressentiment* made palpable.

The feeling of indecency associated with voting is not derived solely from the fact that the choices before one on the ballot may all be indecent, though they may be – who would a decent American have voted for as President in 1964, let alone 1968? Even Lear might be a better sovereign than the blasted Heath government; though the king, himself a poor courtier, would surely forfeit his deposit. But the problem lies deeper than the deficiencies of any set of candidates. Voting may reinvoke the peculiar shame associated with the experience of being a schoolchild. Then, as a means of socialisation, one is repeatedly compelled to take part in false rituals that assert propositions one has not felt to be true and deny others that one has. The purpose, in Laing's terms, is not deception but *mystification*; not to convince the victim of a falsehood but, much more importantly, to convince him that he no longer dare use, or even possesses, the means of learning a usable approximation of the truth. A man who draws the curtain around him to choose between Richard Nixon and Hubert Humphrey has involved himself in a Laingian knot which might be put something like this: an American citizen is proud to live in a country whose policies he can influence by his vote. It is subversive to try to change government policy in any important way, especially if this undermines support for our military commitments or the way private property is distributed. But it is wrong and unpatriotic not to exercise the franchise. Voting, then, must not really affect anything fundamental very much; or it, too, would be considered subversive. It is especially forbidden, however, to consider that voting is either futile or a way of playing the government's game.

To vote, then may make the voter feel as if he had accepted some meaningless badge from an authority he dare not admit that he loathes, like the young George Orwell in 'Such, Such Were the Joys' despising himself for coveting the favour of his headmaster's brutal and silly wife. Refusing to vote is a violation of the pledge, while by the act of voting, the small voice crying 'these are none of them my choices, this is not my way, I am not truly of these people' is effectively stifled. Censorship and surveillance pave the way to the polling place; they cull the material available to instruct the novice in his role in the electoral ceremony by which the integrity of the sovereign state is falsely asserted and reasserted.

'The Americans hold that in every state the supreme power ought to emanate from the people; but when once that power is constituted they can conceive, as it were, no limits to it, and they are ready to admit that it has the right to do whatever it pleases. They have not the slightest notion of peculiar privileges granted to cities, families, or persons; their minds appear never to have forseen that it might be possible not to apply with strict uniformity the same laws to every part of the state and to all its inhabitants.

'These same opinions are more and more diffused in Europe; they even insinuate themselves among those nations that most vehemently reject the principle of the sovereignty of the people. Such nations assign a different origin to the supreme power, but they ascribe to that power the same characteristics. Among them all idea of intermediate powers is weakened and obliterated; the idea of rights inherent in certain individuals is rapidly disappearing from the minds of men; the idea of the omnipotence and sole authority of society at large rises to fill its place. These ideas take root and spread in proportion as social conditions become more equal and men more alike. They are produced by equality, and in turn they hasten the progress of equality.'[8]

The reader will, himself, be able to vouch for the truth of Tocqueville's comments. Nearly 150 years later the idea of a system of government in which different estates possessed, by law as well as custom, different rights and were subject to different restrictions occasions disbelief and bewilderment rather than indignation. Hell, that's unconstitutional! As, indeed, Tocqueville himself pointed out at the time, the entire thrust of history, with steadily increasing force, has been directed towards increased equality throughout its course. This thrust towards equality may, in fact, be the same process as the institutionalisation of the group leading to synthetic reunification of seriality and impotence for the sake of security and social stability which Laing and Sartre discuss. I believe that it is; and from this hypothesis, certain rather striking implications follow.

Since, as Laing and Sartre see it, scarcity is the inescapable pre-condition of alienation and the occasion for the pledge which leads men to begin the process of self-reunification in the interests of the group, the only way to reduce alienation and support is to eliminate scarcity itself. The belief that technology has now made this possible, and that scarcity is a vicious artefact resulting from the built-in inequities of capitalism – an economic system deigned to function under the assumption that scarcity is inevitable and which requires and perpetuates scarcity in order that it may continue to function – has made state socialism an appealing vision, to Sartre and indeed to nearly all contemporary social critics. There is no attractive conservative living and writing at the present in America. Those who are called conservative – Robert Nisbet possibly excepted – are taken for and largely accept themselves as apologists for the existing social order; though that, surely, is the battered wreck of liberalism run rampant.

It is quite true, of course, that the harsh and arbitrary forms of scarcity that enervate and distress modern industrial societies are, indeed, the structural consequences of capitalism and need not occur under socialism – at least, not for structural reasons. The concepts of unemployment and overproduction in a society eroded by dire poverty; the fantasy that people must work at jobs that do not exist, and would serve no useful purpose if they did, in order to justify their sharing in a glut that otherwise goes to waste – such intolerable and arbitrary violations of human need are consequences of capitalism and its underlying ethos; and are sufficient to damn it. But it now appears likely that, even under socialism, scarcity would be engendered through the limitations of technology itself; at least for as long as the memory of what twentieth century America defined as an adequate standard of living dominates the imagination and sets the level of aspiration for mankind the world over. Social justice or no, the people of Bangla-Desh and their billions of counterparts now defined as deprived are not going to get even VWs to drive, or roads to drive them on. They may not always be so proverbially poor that they won't have a pot to piss in – but they won't have one that can be flushed. If everyone in the world had access to these things, they would no longer have air to breathe or water to drink, and there would doubtless be widespread dissatisfaction about that.

There are other possibilities. Ivan Illich, among others, has suggested many; the 'mechanical mule', designed to carry up to 500 pounds of goods or people on bush trails in moderate discomfort at 20 miles an hour; more modest medical establishments designed to foster public health rather than to provide intensive treatment for the aged at costs that only the most affluent can meet. Such proposals would, if they are, as they appear to be, technologically practical, ensure a decent standard of living for the entire world. Or, more precisely, they would eliminate gross squalor and disease during the first fifty years of life, while the standard of living they provide would come to be accepted as what was meant by 'decent'.

It is apparent, however, that this could only happen by institutionalising new forms of constraint to ensure that resources would not be deployed into producing objects or services that could not be universally shared. No more cars, no more jet flights to Paris or Peking, no mention of these things to arouse fruitless aspiration except, perhaps, for those whose administrative responsibilities really required them, and the central committees responsible for judging whether their requirements are really real. As for the people, let them sweep the snow from the streets of Peking by hand as the Presidential Party approaches on its visit, just to show him how high their morale is. They wouldn't do that in New York.

The pledge, it seems, is back; and more active than ever. Alienation is not to be banished by banishing scarcity itself. I would suggest – I have no evidence – that R. D. Laing's recent withdrawal from political activism, preceding his departure for Ceylon, for which he has been roundly criticized by Peter Sedgwick among others, must surely be at least partially attributable to his own growing awareness that this conclusion is implicit in his own argument. It was there all the time; no one who freely and gratefully acknowledges the fundamental influences of Thomas Stearns Eliot on his own thought can in good faith become a left-activist. If I understand R. D. Laing correctly, only the relatively secure are in a position to realize their own freedom and defend that of others. This security is, of course, psychological rather than economic. But psychological security in an open society which rejects ascribed status depends instead on patterns of consumption and job specifications to establish, for the moment, who is who.

The relatively secure are, however, also relatively unlikely to be freedom-lovers. They are already seriously compromised as individuals. They, too, are members of a social group and a narrow one; pledged to see the world through its eyes and keep silent about whatever might trouble its vision; committed to defend such power and affluence as they have against the desperately poor of this world as well as against much more demanding, envious hordes of the relatively affluent. In the past, only a handful of the already small number of the secure have become known as lovers and defenders of freedom; most, as among men of all ranks in life, proved to be its enemies and, granted their positions, among the more powerful of these.

Those who became, instead, its celebrants have usually been marginal members of their own social group. Even when they were not initially, their taste for liberty tended to make them so; but usually they already were. The recipe seems to be something like this: enough experience, preferably early, of personal security to desensitise the unconscious to the threat of scarcity; activated by some kind of stigma, severe enough to loosen the pledge that binds the individual to the group; but not severe enough to get him cast out of group and thus destroy his security. Nor must the stigma be permitted to become *itself* the basis for a new group membership, for this destroys its effectiveness as a bond-weakener; the individual has taken a new pledge and immediately begins to promote his new group-interests at the expense of his scepticism and inner vision. Being Jewish, being black, being gay – all these used to work wonders in establishing marginality, for those who were able to afford it. Today, they avail very little; they are just different ways of getting into politics.

What seems to me to be implied inescapably by Laing's position – though he would surely reject this conclusion himself, if possible – is that freedom and self-realization have always been, and must remain, the concerns of an elite of some kind, self-defined by its very nature as an enemy of the people. If it is not to become merely another group, obsessed and corrupted by the demands of its own defence, then, clearly, it must be relatively invulnerable for reasons with which it need not concern itself too much from day to day. Wealth helps, but capitalism has done a superb job of defining wealth in such a way that nobody ever seems sure he has enough and can keep it, especially in a state made fretful by an uneasy social conscience. The national conscience has enough to be fretful about. Yet humaneness derived from guilt is about as trustworthy as chastity imposed by gonorrhea. Neither is evidence of a change of heart.

If my reasoning is correct, then demands for a just society, as social justice is now conceived, must continue to conflict very sharply with the demand for personal self-realisation. I am not here referring at all to individual competitive achievement or success – quite the contrary. Obviously, the most militantly egalitarian state provides plenty of opportunity for that, though defined in different terms from those North Americans easily accept. I am referring rather to the conflict between social justice and inwardness. And inwardness is necessary, though insufficient, to the development of authenticity.

It is currently fashionable to put down the 'pot-left' or 'freak-left' as a political embarrassment to true radicals. The counter-culture is seen as a drag to the revolution; its hair and its egotism alienate the working class; its 'free schools' delay the kind of hard-nosed educational reform needed to lift children out of the ghetto and politicise their parents. All this is true; and it is not inappropriate that a counter-culture be counter-revolutionary. But the counter-culture is in deeper conflict with the dominant culture of our time, whether in East or West, than any current revolutionary movement conceived in political or military form.

This conflict, though profoundly political in its implications, is really metapolitical. It transcends politics, since the counter-cultural position perceives political action as alienating in itself. As Thomas à Becket came to understand in T. S. Eliot's portrayal of him,

> ... those who serve the greater cause may make the cause serve them,
> Still doing right: and striving with political men
> May make that cause political, not by what they do
> But by what they are.

This is not to imply that men ought not to fight evil and social injustice. They very often must, but when they must, the price is their own objectification – their conversion, by their own consent but in ways they can seldom have anticipated, or wholly come to accept, into an instrument of social action. The extreme case is represented by the character called Churchill in Hochuth's *Soldiers*; but even the most sympathetic political figures hardly hope to escape.

Whatever his personal politics may be, the thrust of Ronald Laing's work, as well as much of its substance, has been the very stuff of the counter-culture's vision. The old friend of Baba Ram Dass and Timothy Leary has never betrayed their joint ideal. It is finally no paradox, but a near classic example of the relationship between *yang* and *yin*, that his prophetic insights into the political character of, first, mental illness, then, of experience should have led Ronald Laing to a position from which politics itself can only be seen as absurd. The position is stated precisely by Laing himself, in the final paragraphs of his moving and fantastic essay, *The Bird of Paradise*:

There is really nothing more to say when we come back to that beginning of all beginnings that is nothing at all. Only when you begin to lose that Alpha and Omega do you want to start to talk and to write, and then there is no end to it, words, words, words. At best and most they are perhaps *in memoriam*, evocations, conjurations, incantations, emanations, shimmering, iridescent flares in the sky of darkness, a just still feasible tact, indiscretions, perhaps forgivable. . . .*

City lights at night, from the air, receding, like these words, atoms each containing its own world and every other world. Each a fuse to set you off. . . .*

If I could turn you on, if I could drive you out of your wretched mind, If I could tell you I would let you know.[9]

* Ellipses in original.

Notes

1. THE MYTH OF MENTAL ILLNESS, pp. 7-31

1. Though *The Divided Self* was not published until 1959, Laing notes in the Preface that 'the clinical work upon which these studies are based was all completed before 1956.... Since the book was completed in 1957 it has been read by many people....' In the Preface to the Penguin edition, Laing states, 'I wrote this book when I was twenty-eight.'
2. *The Politics of the Family*. London: Tavistock Publications, 1971, p. 41.
3. In Chapter 5, 'The Schizophrenic Experience' of *The Politics of Experience*. Harmondsworth: Penguin Books, 1967, p. 101.
4. Harmondsworth: Penguin Books, 1970.
5. This, too, would of course be denied – *is* explicitly denied – by those who think of physical illness as an expression of imbalance both organic and spiritual. Vitamin C is the particular target of animadversion by practitioners of Zen Macrobiotics, who perceive it as excessively *yin* in its action. Thus Neven Hanaff, in a pamphlet called 'Vitamin C' (macroguide no. 6: San Francisco, The George Ohsawa Macrobiotic Foundation, n.d., pp. 6-14) asserts that 'MODERN DOCTORS LEND CREDENCE TO A GROSS MISCONCEPTION BY AFFIRMING THAT SCURVY IS CAUSED BY THE ABSENCE OF VITAMIN C IN FOODS' (capitalization his). Hanaff maintains that, since adequate amounts of vitamin C to sustain life are synthesized by the bodies of humans who are otherwise healthy, to attribute scurvy to insufficient *intake* of vitamin C in foods is comparable to attributing diabetes to a failure to take injections of insulin; both are due to a prior biological maladjustment.

Whatever the merits of this position, it is certainly worth considering as pertinent to the internal consistency of Laing's view of illness, which has continually become more transcendental and in some respects specifically Buddhist; and more determined in its rejection of the 'disorienting' effects of the approach and the metaphysic of Western empirical medicine.

6. G. Bateson, D. D. Jackson, J. Haley, and J. Weakland, 'Toward a Theory of Schizophrenia'. *Behavioural Science*, 1, 251, 1956
7. New York, 1970, p. 90.
8. London : Faber and Faber, 1950.
9. In an interview with Peter Mezan, *Esquire*, January 1972, p. 17.
10. Flannery O'Connor, *A Good Man is Hard to Find*. London : Faber and Faber, 1958.

2. MADNESS AND POLICY, pp. 32–56

1. 'After Freud and Jung, Now Comes R. D. Laing Pop-Shrink, Rebel, Philosopher-King? Latest Reincarnation of Aesculapius, Maybe,' January, 1972, p. 171 *et seq.*
2. *Ibid.* p. 174.
3. *Ibid.* p. 176.
4. *Ibid.* p. 174.
5. *The New York Times*, October 7, 1972, p. 37.
6. 'On Being Sane in Insane Places.' *Science*, 179, 4070, pp. 250–58, 19 January 1973.

3. LAING'S RELATIONSHIP TO PHILOSOPHY, pp. 57–96

1. London : Tavistock Publications, 1964.
2. Included in Robert Boyers and Robert Orrill, Editors, *R. D. Laing and Anti-Psychiatry*. New York : Harper & Row, 1971, p. 11.
3. *Reason and Violence*, p. 115.
4. London : Tavistock Publications, 1967.
5. Rollo May, Ernest Angel, and Henri F. Ellenberger, Editors, *Existence*. New York : Basic Books, 1958, p. 11. Italics in original
6. *Ibid.* p. 50.
7. May *et al., op cit.,* pp. 50–51.
8. This is not a paradox; but a basic convention of social organization. Morale in the armed forces, for example, depends on precisely this device. Because the soldier's self-image is linked to his unit and to the image of himself as normally courageous, he will become more anxious if he abandons his buddies and seeks safety; less anxious if he goes into battle at their side. To make assurance doubly sure, deserters may be shot, but this is probably unnecessary and may even be counterproductive if the threat arouses enough resentment to cause disloyalty.
9. New York : The Free Press, 1967, *passim.*

10. *The Self and Others.* London: Tavistock Publications, 1961, p. 56.
11. Originally published as 'Der Fall Ellen West'. *Schweitzer Archiv für Neurologie und Psychiatrie*, 1944, Vol. 53, pp. 255–277; Vol. 54, pp. 69–117, 330–360; 1945, Vol. 55, pp. 16–40. The case, then, had been published 14 years earlier than *Existence*.
12. *The Divided Self*, p. 38n.
13. May *et al.. op. cit.*, p. 345.
14. *Ibid.* p. 267.
15. From *Two Cheers for Democracy.* London: Edward Arnold, 1951, pp. 83–84.

4. SOME IMPLICATIONS OF LAING'S PHILOSOPHICAL POSITION, pp. 97–120.

1. Friedrich Nietzsche, *The Birth of Tragedy* and *The Genealogy of Morals*, Francis Golffing trans., Garden City, New York: Anchor Books, 1956. The concept of *Ressentiment*, which Golffing translates as rancor, is developed in the latter work.
2. Max Scheler, *Ressentiment*, William W. Holdheim, trans., Glencoe, Illinois: The Free Press, 1961, pp. 45–46.
3. Hazel E. Barnes, trans., London: Methuen, 1969.
4. New York: Norton, 1957, pp. 15–18 (Italics in original).
5. *Ibid.* p. 16.
6. New York: Oxford University Press, 1956, p. 301.
7. New York: Random House, 1945. Vol. II, p. 259 (originally published in 1840).
8. Tocqueville, *op. cit.*, pp. 307–8.
9. *The Politics of Experience* and *The Bird of Paradise.* Harmondsworth: Penguin Books, 1967, p. 156.

Books and Selected Articles
by Laing and Others

Bateson, G., Jackson, D. D., Haley, J., Weakland, J. 'Toward a Theory of Schizophrenia', *Behavioral Science*, 1, 251, 1956.

Bettelheim, Bruno. *The Divided Self*. New York: The Free Press, 1967.

Boyers, Robert, and Orrill, Robert. *R. D. Laing and Anti-Psychiatry*. New York: Harper and Row, 1971

Eliot, T. S. *The Cocktail Party*. London: Faber and Faber, 1950.

Eliot, T. S. *Murder in the Cathedral*. London: Faber and Faber, 1935.

Foucault, Michel. *Madness and Civilization*. London: Tavistock Publications, 1967.

Forster, E. M. *Two Cheers for Democracy*. London: Edward Arnold, 1951.

Glass, James M. 'Schizophrenia and Perception: a critique of the liberal theory of externality', *Inquiry*, 15, 1972, pp. 114–45.

Goffman, Erving. *Asylums*. Harmondsworth: Penguin Books, 1970.

Laing, Ronald D. *The Divided Self*. London: Tavistock Publications, 1959; Penguin Books.

Laing, Ronald D. *Knots*. London: Tavistock Publications, 1970.

Laing, Ronald D. *The Politics of Experience*. Harmondsworth: Penguin Books, 1967.

Laing, Ronald D. *The Politics of the Family*. London: Tavistock Publications, 1971.

Laing, Ronald D. and Cooper, David. *Reason and Violence*. London: Tavistock Publications, 1964.

Laing, Ronald D. and Esterson, A. *Sanity, Madness and the Family*. London: Tavistock Publications, 1964; Penguin Books.

Laing, Ronald D. *The Self and Others*. London: Tavistock Publications, 1961; Penguin Books.

May, Rollo, Angel, Ernest, and Ellenberger, Henri F., editors. *Existence*. New York: Basic Books, 1958.

Mezan, Peter. 'After Freud and Jung, Now Comes R. D. Laing Pop-shrink Rebel, Yogi, Philosopher-King, Latest Reincarnation of Aesculapius, Maybe', *Esquire*, January, 1972, p. 171 *et seq.*

Mills, Wright C. *The Power Elite*. New York: Oxford University Press, 1956.

Nietzsche, Friedrich. *The Genealogy of Morals*. (Francis Golffing, tr.) New York: Anchor, 1956.

Ortega y Gasset, Jose. *The Revolt of the Masses*. New York: Norton, 1959.

Rogers, Carl. *Counseling and Psychotherapy: Newer Concepts in Practice*. Boston: Houghton Mifflin, 1942.

Rogers, Carl. *On Becoming a Person*. Boston: Houghton Mifflin, 1961.

Sartre, J. P. *Being and Nothingness*. (Hazel Barnes, tr.) London: Methuen, 1969.

Sartre, J. P. *Critique de la Raison Dialectique*. Paris: Gallimard, 1960.

Scheler, May. *Ressentiment*. (W. N. Holdheim, tr.) Glencoe, Ill.: The Free Press, 1961.

Schickel, R. 'The Truth Which Dares not Speak its Name', *Harpers*, 242, 104–8, April 1971.

Sennett, Richard, *New York Times Book Review*. 'The Politics of the Family.' Nov. 28, p. 54 et seq.

Sullivan, H. S. *The Interpersonal Theory of Psychiatry*. New York: Norton, 1953.

Szasz, Thomas S. *Ideology and Insanity: Essays on the Psychiatric Dehumanization of Man*. Garden City, New York: Anchor, 1970.

Szasz, Thomas S. *Law, Liberty and Psychiatry: An Inquiry into the Social Uses of Mental Health Practices*. New York: Macmillan, 1968.

Szasz, Thomas S. *The Manufacture of Madness: A Comparative Study of the Inquisition and the Mental Health Movement*. London: Routledge, 1972.

Szasz, Thomas S. *The Myth of Mental Illness: Foundations of a Theory of Personal Conduct*. London: Paladin Books, 1972.

Tocqueville, de Alexis. *Democracy in America*. New York: Random House, 1945 (originally published 1840).

Vonnegut, Kurt. *Cat's Cradle*. London: Gollancz, 1971.

Some Fontana Modern Masters

By the end of 1973, 24 titles had been published in this steadily growing series, edited by Frank Kermode, Lord Northcliffe Professor of Modern English Literature at University College, London.

Each book presents a clear, concise and authoritative introduction to the life and work of a man who has changed and is changing the life and thought of our age. The authors are themselves distinguished contemporary writers and thinkers, for whom their subject has some particular importance. Each book includes a biographical chronology of the 'modern master' and an up-to-date bibliography of his work.

Gandhi George Woodcock
'One of the best accounts yet printed of Mahatma's life and his techniques of revolution . . .' Cyril Dunn, *The Observer Review*

Lenin Robert Conquest
'Intelligent, gracefully written, and far removed from the baleful style of Cold War polemic which used to make short books on Communist problems such gloomy reading.'
Neal Ascherson, *The Observer*

Popper Bryan Magee
'Lucid, based on close study and deep understanding, the perfect pocket guide to a thinker whose importance it is impossible to overestimate.' Bernard Levin, *The Observer*

Yeats Denis Donoghue
'Professor Donoghue, casting a cool if not iconoclastic eye, isolates with perception and elegance, the central preoccupations of the poetry and thought.' *The Times*

Memories, Dreams, Reflections

C. G. Jung

Until near the end of his long life, Jung steadfastly refused to attempt the autobiography which his friends and disciples urged him to write and his admirers throughout the world hoped for from him. What he had to say, he maintained, was to be found in the twenty volumes of his professional writings. However, in 1957 he agreed to provide his friend and assistant of many years standing, Aniela Jaffe, with the necessary material and exercise a responsible supervision over what she wrote. Soon the task so fascinated him that he began doing the writing himself; and the manuscript as he left it on his death in 1961 is very largely from his own hand. The result is a unique memoir of the inner life of a great and original genius.

'Jung's single-minded humility, his passion to unearth truth, is one of the loveliest impressions to emerge from this absorbing and many-sided book.' *The Times*

'He was on a giant scale . . . he was a master of the soul in his insights, a profound sage in his conclusions. He is also one of Western Man's great liberators.' J. B. Priestley, *Sunday Telegraph*

'Can sometimes rise to the heights of a Blake or a Nietzsche or a Kierkegaard . . . like any true prophet or artist extended the range of the human imagination . . . to be able to share Jungian emotions is surely an almost necessary capacity of the free mind.' Philip Toynbee, *Observer*

A Fontana Selection

L's Rhetoric